Embracing
THE END-TIME HARVEST

Embracing
THE END-TIME HARVEST

Be Strengthened to Disciple Others
OLIVIA MCCLURE

Printed in Canada

ISBN: 978-1-4866-1596-4

Word Alive Press
119 De Baets Street, Winnipeg, MB R2J 3R9
www.wordalivepress.ca

MIX
Paper from
responsible sources
FSC® C016245

Cataloguing in Publication may be obtained through Library and Archives Canada

Dedication

To my children, grandchildren, and to the generations to come.

To those who have impacted my life, including my parents, who taught me the introductory tenets of faith in Jesus Christ. I will always remember and uphold them with honour.

To my Bible teachers and mentors, and my pastors, Faisal and Sabina Malick, who have impacted my life. I have had the privilege and honour to get to know their heart and vision, God's vision.

I must also dedicate this book to Holy Spirit who has been a constant guide, mentor, and encourager throughout my spiritual journey and now in the writing of this book. To Jesus the Son of God, the head of the Body of Christ. Also, our heavenly Father who has expressed to me His unfathomable and unchanging love.

—Olivia McClure

Content

Preface

I would like to introduce you to Olivia McClure and congratulate her on the release of her new book, *Embracing the End Time Harvest*. Filled with practical wisdom and real-life experiences this book is a great resource for any believer or new disciple of Christ.

—Faisal Malick
Lead Pastor of Covenant of Life Ministries
President of Plumbline Network
www.plumblinenetwork.com

Introduction

To everything there is a season, A time for every purpose under heaven.
—Ecclesiastes 3:1

God has a plan in place for every generation since the beginning, but many of us have blinders over our eyes, keeping us from seeing God's awesome plan for humanity.

He invites us to cooperate with Him in accomplishing His plan. A remnant from each generation have said yes. Those people have played out their part in God's awesome plan for His creation, a plan made before the foundation of the world.

But how do we know what that plan is?

God has left us His inspired Word, the Bible. The Bible is more than another history book. It is the inspired Word of God through which the Holy Spirit convicts and teaches generations to respond to His call so that they by faith we might receive His gift of eternal life through Jesus Christ. He is the only hope for the hopeless and the weary.

This is called the gospel, or good news. The news is that Jesus Christ willingly spilled His perfect sinless blood, and died for all, so you and I would not have to. Just over two thousand years ago, Jesus came through the virgin birth of Mary. Mary in the Bible made it possible by her willingness to conceive, when Holy Spirit impregnated her. Thirty-three years later, Jesus gave His life, and rose from the dead three days later. This is heavenly Father's highest expression of love. All past, present, and future sins are under the blood, never to be remembered again. It was accomplished once, and for all.

This message is not something we keep to ourselves, but is meant to be shared with peoples of all nations, cultures, and generations. In fact, in the Bible, God commands us to go out and share it with the people around us, and around the world:

> *Preach the word! Be ready in season and out of season. Convince, rebuke, exhort, with all longsuffering and teaching. For the time will come when they will not endure sound doctrine, but according to their own desires, because they have itching ears, they will heap up for themselves teachers; and they will turn their ears away from the truth, and be turned aside to fables. But you be watchful in all things, endure afflictions, do the work of an evangelist, fulfill your ministry.*
>
> —2 Timothy 4:2–5

I used to get offended when people said to me, "You're nothing but a religious fanatic." Now I don't get offended because people who say this don't know the Word of God, and they speak with a lack of understanding. What God wants is not religion but for us to have a personal relationship with Jesus Christ the Son of God—this relationship and religion are opposites. Remember one thing: it was the religious crowd who killed Jesus. They did not believe, nor will many people believe, that Jesus is the Messiah, the Son of God. He is the Promised One who was prophesied thousands of years before. Historical records that prove this point have been protected in God's Word. Sin has blinded and deafened us to this truth, but things are changing and deliverance is coming for those who choose to hear and see. The blinders are coming off spiritual eyes. (I say, "Thank you Holy Spirit for preparing the spiritual soil of many hearts who will yet to come into this awesome kingdom of God for such a time as this.")

But we each have a choice. We can choose to believe God's Word, the message of faith, hope and love—or not. We can say, "I will love and obey Jesus Christ the Son of God, who is the head of the church." I have made that choice and I pray you will choose this too. Whether these ideas are brand new to you, or you are a new believer, or someone who has been on this journey for a few years, my prayer is that as you read this book you will be strengthened and built up in your most holy faith (Jude 1:20).

So let's get started!

Prophetic Word of the Lord

As I was spending time in prayer and reading His Word on December 11, 2015, this is what I heard the Holy Spirit say to me:

"I am raising up a people, a remnant who are consumed with God's love, presence, vision, and purposes. It's like a fire that's burning strong, and it consumes and burns up anything that does not resemble Me.

"The fire that burns is like the white light of My glory. I am raising up a people with a corporate anointing that will sweep over the earth. It is an anointing that breaks the yokes of bondage. It is an anointing that totally delivers a people and sets them on a path declaring the goodness and greatness of God.

"Millions will take up the Cross, and follow Me. For I have been sent by the Father as a deliverer. I have made it possible, for I have redeemed you from the old life through my shed blood, death and resurrection. My love permits you to embrace the new life which provides My peace, My joy and My righteousness. For My voice is like thunder; it is like lightning, precise and clear and powerful. My voice is not only speaking, but calling you for this season which is upon you. Come!

"The container of My glory and power is expanding. It is like a city set on a hill, shining for all to see. For the river that flows out of this city has one mind, My mind. It has one purpose, My purpose; it has one heart, My heart. Every person it touches brings forth life and hope. For the people in the world will know you are My disciples because you have love one for another. My love that is eternal has penetrated and is increasing as you shine forth like pure gold, that is to say like My divine nature."

CHAPTER ONE
The Building of Excellent Things

IN THE BEGINNING GOD CREATED THE HEAVENS AND THE EARTH, BUT THIS WAS not the end of his building. Many stories in the Bible have to do with building and many stories in the Bible are mentioned from Genesis to Revelation.

- A new city, a new temple (Ezekiel 40–46)
- Noah built an ark (Genesis 6)
- Moses built a tabernacle (Exodus 35)
- David built a tabernacle (2 Samuel 6; 1 Chronicles 16; Psalm 15; Amos 9; Acts 15)
- Solomon built a temple (1 Kings 5)

A thread of building runs all the way through Scripture. God uses building as a picture for what He is doing in us: the Bible teaches us that we are a dwelling place for the Lord and that the foundation of our lives are established as the Holy Spirit builds it:

For every house is built by someone, but He who built all things is God. And Moses indeed was faithful in all His house as a servant, for a testimony of those things which would be spoken afterward, but Christ as a Son over His own house, whose house we are if we hold fast the confidence and the rejoicing of the hope firm to the end.

—Hebrews 3:4–6

See 1 Corinthians 3:9–17; 1 Corinthians 6:19–20; Hebrew 3:6; John 14; Ephesians 2:22 for more examples of God building people.

When Jesus was growing up, he hung around his father, Joseph, who was a carpenter (Matthew 13; Mark 6) who built out of wood. Jesus' heavenly father builds a people for Himself. Why? God desires a dwelling place, an eternal residence. This building is unique because you and I have each been made a particular way for His purpose. This building is so beautiful because it is comprised of His creation.

A home I lived in helps me understand what God is doing. Many years ago when we purchased our cedar home, we had the fun of resurrecting it. When my husband picked up our prefabricated home, he had to number every log and every wall so when it was time to put it all together, it would come together, just the way it was created to be. The building engineers had an architectural plan, so every part fit perfectly. When we put the walls back together, we had to make sure we had exactly the correct log fitting in with the log below it. There was a pattern and proper order required. There was no room for a mistake. My husband and son popped the logs in with a rubber mallet.

Each four–inch log that made up the walls and ceiling was joined together through the dynamics of the tongue and groove method. Even the open beam ceiling has cedar tongue and groove boards fitly joining together. It is probably one of the most solid homes in our city.

Every log has a very important part to play. Not one log looks exactly the same as any other but it complements the other logs. There is a warmth about this house because of the cedar. In fact, cedar is used in wainscoting for more warmth. There is no extra insulation, except between the ceiling and the roof. It has a protection element within it: cedar does not rot, and bugs do not attack it.

In the Strong's Concordance, Hebrew original, cedar means: firm from the strength of its roots. In the Bible, cedar wood was very valuable. It still is: when we purchased some two–inch mouldings for the house in 1992, it was very costly.

Cedar also has many healing properties and scientists studying essential oils have discovered many uses and benefits of cedar oil.

Similarly, God places high value on you and me. And just as there are no spacers between each log and nothing can come between the logs that are fitly joined together, so it is with the building God is preparing: the love of God holds us together so that no prejudice, no hatred, no jealousy, no pride can slip in. We are all equal and valuable. We support one another. And, just as cedar has a wonderful smell, so the Apostle Paul says:

> *Therefore be imitators of God as dear children. And walk in love, as Christ also has loved us and given Himself for us, an offering and a sacrifice to God for a sweet–smelling aroma.*

> —Ephesians 5:1–2

Not that I seek the gift, but I seek the fruit that abounds to your account. Indeed, I have all and abound. I am full, having received from Epaphroditus the things sent from you, a sweet–smelling aroma, an acceptable sacrifice, well pleasing to God.

—Philippians 4:17–18

I use these examples to specifically help you see the spiritual building God is building for Himself. He is putting the finishing touches on it. This is His home, His dwelling place.

Before the foundation of the world, God already had planned which family you would be in, which church family you would be in years ago, and the one you are in at the moment, or the one you are going to be in. He makes no mistakes. You are not a mistake (Acts 2:46).

God uses many images to describe us—for instance, Isaiah 64:8 says we are the clay and He is the potter—but He often uses the image of us being a house. Perhaps the best news is found in 2 Corinthians 5:1–8 where God says, we have a building from God, a house not made with hands, one that will be eternal in the heavens.

ADDITIONAL READING: Hebrews 3:5–6; 1 Peter 2:1–5; Zechariah 6:12–13; Matthew 4:5; Matthew 21:12–13; 1 Corinthians 3:6; 1 Corinthians 6:19; 2 Corinthians 6:16; Ephesians 2:21; John 14:2, 23; Revelation 21:3, 9–27; Galatians 4:19; Exodus 25:9, 40; Hebrews 8:7–9:14; Titus 2:7; 1 Timothy 1:12–17.

CHAPTER TWO
The Natural Versus the Spiritual

WHEN YOU WERE BORN, YOUR MOTHER DID NOT DELIVER A MATURE ADULT. You were a tiny baby, and it took time for you to grow up. The same is true when you are born again spiritually: you are not instantly transformed into a fully mature spiritual person—it takes time to grow (1 Corinthians 15:44, 46). And just as babies are first fed milk and then given solid food, you feed from the milk of the Word until you are able to receive the solid spiritual food (Isaiah 28:9–11; 1 Corinthians 3:2; Hebrews 5:12–13; 1 Peter 2:2). A spiritual father in the faith wrote something that resonated with me: "To live is to grow, to grow is to change. Spiritual growth denotes change after change after change." We can also see this principle in 2 Corinthians 3:18.

Just as you have a family lineage (ancestry), you also have a spiritual lineage and that was Abraham, our father in the faith.

When you were born into your natural family, you took on the DNA of your parents; when you are born again into the spiritual family of God, your spirit took on the DNA of God. This is the difference between the natural and the spiritual, the earthly and the heavenly, the kingdom of darkness and the kingdom of light. There is a natural temple (your body) and there is a spiritual temple (spiritual body).

God said in the beginning, "*Let us make man in our image*" (Genesis 1:26) and later "*God is spirit and those who worship Him must worship Him in spirit and in truth*" (John 4:24). Just as God is three in one (Father, Son and Holy Spirit), so we are three in one (spirit, soul, and body). Many people in the world focus on their bodies or their skills and talents. Those things have value, but many people do not consider or even know they are a three–part being: they forget about their spirit which has been alienated from God because of sin coming into the world.

The good news is that although sin alienates us from God, God had a plan before the foundation of this world so He could redeem us from sin unto righteousness. How? He sent His Son Jesus to pay for all our sins, past, present and future (Hebrews 9:11–12; Hebrews 7:27). Jesus was a human being just like you and me, but He still remained God. The Old Testament gave a picture of what God would do through Jesus, the new covenant that would pay the penalty for our sins so that we could have fellowship with God just like Adam and Eve did before they fell through disobedience.

God, through Jesus and His finished work, promises us a new resurrected and new created spirit. When you invite Jesus to come in and abide within you, He immediately gives you a brand new spirit, with new DNA. Now old things are passed away, and all things become absolutely brand new. Your old nature died when Jesus died, was buried, and when Jesus arose, you received a new nature with the resurrection power that raised Jesus from the dead. How is that possible? Because you invited Jesus Christ who is Spirit into your spirit and immediately you are no longer the same person you were before you invited Him into your life. Now this is the miracle, when you invited Him in by faith (2 Corinthians 5:17; Galatians 2:20).

Some people may never have taken this step. But the Bible says clearly: "...*unless one is born again, he cannot see the kingdom of God*" (John 3:3). If you have never entered into this relationship, here is a prayer you can pray so that you have this new spirit and new nature:

Dear Heavenly Father,
Thank you for sending your Son Jesus that I may come alive spiritually. Thank You, Jesus, for your obedience when You shed Your blood, that perfect sacrifice, and that You were buried, and arose again on the third day. You say in Your Word that when you were buried I was buried, and the old nature died. When you arose in resurrection life and power, I arose

with you. I am forever grateful. I choose to be a willing and obedient follower of You, Jesus. Thank you for expressing Yourself through the Holy Spirit who has come to live in my heart forever. I thank you and acknowledge that you are Jesus, the Son of God. Amen.

Others may say, "How come I don't feel like I have this changed life? I still think like I did?" My response to that Satan is a liar and is defeated but he still tries to persuade us we have not changed, using lies and suggestions (Romans 7:22–23). This is just a memory. Also Scripture tells us, "...*But we have the mind of Christ*" (1 Corinthians 2:16). As we study the Word of God and believe it by faith, we received the gift of salvation and were positioned in the heavenly realm. Later, you will discover what your inheritance truly is. It is so awesome. As you begin to live your faith out, the thought of even wanting to sin will dissipate.

Paul says, "...*I labor in birth again until Christ is formed in you*" (Galatians 4:19). Remember this: you are on a journey of continuous growth; spiritual growth involves change after change.

ADDITIONAL READING: Romans 1:17; Hebrews 11:1–10; Acts 15:9; Acts 20:18–21; Romans 5:1–2; Romans 10:17; Romans 12:3; 2 Corinthians 5:7.

CHAPTER THREE

Jesus, the King of Kings

WE WORSHIP AN AWESOME KING WHO LAYS SUCH HONOUR UPON THOSE OF us who believe. Friend, read these verses to understand our inheritance:

Lord, you have been our dwelling place in all generations. Before the mountains were brought forth, or ever You had formed the earth and the world, even from everlasting to everlasting, You are God.

—Psalm 90:1–2

In the beginning was the Word, and the Word was with God, and the Word was God. He was in the beginning with God. All things were made through Him, and without Him nothing was made that was made. In Him was life, and the life was the light of men. And the light shines in the darkness, and the darkness did not comprehend it.

—John 1:1–5

Blessed be the God and Father of our Lord Jesus Christ, who has blessed us with every spiritual blessing in the heavenly places in Christ, just as He chose us in Him before the foundation of the world, that we should be holy and without blame before Him in love, having predestined us to adoption as sons by Jesus Christ to Himself, according to the good pleasure of His will, to the praise of the glory of His grace, by which He made us accepted in the Beloved. In Him we have redemption through His blood, the forgiveness of sins, according to the riches of His grace which He made to abound toward us in all wisdom and prudence, having made known to us the mystery of His will, according to His good pleasure which He purposed in Himself, that in the dispensation of the fullness of the times He might gather together in one all things in Christ, both which are in heaven and which are on earth—in Him. In Him also we have obtained an inheritance, being predestined according to the purpose of Him who works all things according to the counsel of His will, that we who first trusted in Christ should be to the praise of His glory. In Him you also trusted, after you heard the word of truth, the gospel of your salvation; in whom also, having believed, you were sealed with the Holy Spirit of promise, who is the guarantee of our inheritance until the redemption of the purchased possession, to the praise of His glory.

—Ephesians 1: 3–14

God's plan is high above our plans. His thoughts are so far above ours. King Jesus is the plan for His grace to be expressed, His joy, His redemptive work, His restoration, His love, His mercy. Just think about it: God chose to attach us as His Body; to the Head, who is Jesus Christ, King of Kings and Lord of Lords. To have a kingdom, God chose to create humankind for His pleasure to have an intricate part in ruling this kingdom.

To have a kingdom you need a king. The king of this kingdom was known long before He came onto the scene through the virgin birth of Jesus.

The psalmist David exalted and glorified the King of Kings in his season. It was revealed to David that one day the Messiah would come. This King would rule after the order of Melchizedek, king of Salem, priest of the Most High God (see Hebrews 7:1, 3).

As I look at David the king in the Psalms, his heart and posture are turned toward the coming Messiah, our King. Through David, God spoke prophetically about King Jesus, the Messiah who would come to redeem the nations for His inheritance. In Psalm 2: 6–8, David says:

Yet I have set My King on My holy hill of Zion. I will declare the decree: The LORD has said to Me, "You are My Son, Today I have begotten You. Ask of Me, and I will give You The nations for Your inheritance, And the ends of the earth for Your possession."

We see this fulfilled in Acts 13:33–39.

We see other prophecies from the Psalms confirmed in the New Testament. Here are some examples:

Psalms 8:6 & Hebrews 2:6–10	Psalm 41:9 & John 13:18
Psalms 16:10 & Acts 2:27	Psalm 45:6 & Hebrews 1:8
Psalms 22:1 & Matthew 27:46	Psalm 69:9 & John 2:17
Psalms 22:8 & Matthew 27:43	Psalm 109:8 & Acts 1:20
Psalms 22:16 & John 20:25	Psalm 110:1 & Matthew 22:44
Psalms 22:18 & John 19:24	Psalm 110:4 & Hebrews 7:17
Psalms 31:5 & Luke 23:46	Psalm 118:22, 26 &
Psalms 40: 8 & Hebrews 10:7	Matthew 21: 9, 42

David so beautifully describes the coming Messiah, Jesus, the King of Kings. In Psalms 144 and 145, you will discover the attributes of our King Jesus, who is described as: my rock, lovingkindness, fortress, my stronghold, deliverer, my shield, my refuge, unsearchable greatness, our abundant goodness, our righteousness, gracious, merciful, all powerful, a majestic kingdom, everlasting kingdom, dominion that endures forever, our sustainer, supplier, kindness, one who draws near to all who call upon Him in truth, one who fulfills all the desires of those who fear Him, saviour, and keeper of all who love Him.

We can get really excited about and embrace these attributes. Jesus who is the King of Kings and who cannot lie promises all of this to all who love Him. Wow! What a mighty God. He is a well of living water that will never run dry for all eternity. You are standing in eternity now. Why? You have an eternal spirit.

If David can experience such an awesome relationship with our King before the cross, how about we who live after the cross? You just cannot lose. God is so worth it.

Take time now to ponder and meditate on who our King is. Respond to Him with your expression of praise, love, joy, gladness, adoration, thankfulness, gratefulness, and appreciation. It's good to speak out loud your heart to the King.

David was not the only one to prophesy about the King of Kings. Let's take a look at another prophet of the Lord, Isaiah, around 735 BC, who had a vision and a calling that was life–changing for him.

In his vision, Isaiah saw the Lord, sitting on a throne, high and lifted up, and His train filled the temple. This train was like a skirt that spread throughout the whole temple. This was an expression of God's presence, His holiness (purity), His glory, majesty and power. He also saw seraphim (creatures of the angelic realm) who each had six wings that covered God's face and His feet. The brightness could not be looked at directly but was overshadowed by these wings (for more on this, see Revelation 1:12–20). As these seraphim flew around, they said to each other, *"Holy, holy, holy is the Lord of Hosts; the whole earth is full of His glory"* (Isaiah 6:3). The posts of the temple shook, and the house was filled with smoke.

In this vision, Isaiah's spiritual eyes were opened and his response was to cry out:

Woe is me, for I am undone! Because I am a man of unclean lips, and I dwell in the midst of a people of unclean lips; For my eyes have seen the King, The LORD of hosts.

—Isaiah 6:5

God sent an angel to take Isaiah's sin away. Then Isaiah heard a call from the Lord. *"'Whom shall I send, And who will go for Us?'"* (Isaiah 6:8) And Isaiah replied, *"'Here am I! Send me'"* (Isaiah 6:8).

Embracing the end–time harvest requires us to hear that call, and to go out with a changed heart, a changed mind, and the compassion of the Father. We need to see with His eyes and His heart for a lost and dying generation who need to come into the kingdom of God.

I sensed God's call years ago. My family and I were living in the Lower Mainland of British Columbia during the late '70s. One morning after my husband had gone to work and my children had gone to school, I felt an urgency to get down on my knees in front of the coffee table of our living room. I began to pray. I prayed in English and then I prayed in the heavenly language. After a short period of time, I had an overwhelming and tangible sense of the presence of God in the room. Every moment that it lasted, I felt as though I must crawl under the coffee table. The problem was that the bottom of the coffee table was only about an inch off the ground. I thought if I could only crawl under the rug, somehow I could handle this powerful presence of God. As I lay flat out on the floor, I heard myself speak out loud, "I am undone, I am unclean, please forgive me." The fear of God was so strong in the room that I felt I could not take another second of it or my body would split apart. After I spoke these words to the Lord, I sensed the weightiness of His presence and holiness of God. The Love He expressed to me, I cannot describe in words. That moment was life–changing, and I knew something had changed. I sensed His overwhelming love. I beheld God's glory as King of Kings.

Not long afterwards, a prophetic ministry came to our local assembly for a conference. What I remember about the prophecy was that some of us would be sent out like arrows to places that needed hope and to experience the Lord. These would be dark places, places I would have never dreamed of. Within a few years of that time, both my husband and I felt a leading to move into the interior of British Columbia. It was then our story began to unfold with all manner of zigs and zags, but the Lord brought life to our story. They were growing times, but also powerful times as the Lord led us to different places of ministry. We were honoured to see quite a number of people give their heart to the Lord, bringing discipleship to many. We saw the miracles of God: casting out of demons, laying hands on the sick who recovered, people filled with the Holy Spirit and speaking in other tongues just like on the day of Pentecost. Was it always easy? Of course not. I learned one thing, God's grace was there to see us through. God was more than faithful. I give all the glory to Jesus, the King of Kings.

CHAPTER FOUR
The Kingdom of God

WHEN WAS THE LAST TIME YOU RECITED THE LORD'S PRAYER (MATTHEW 6:9–13)? Most of you reading this will have either recited the prayer at school or perhaps in a church service. Let's say it now:

> *Our Father in heaven,*
> *Hallowed be Your name.*
> *Your kingdom come.*
> *Your will be done*
> *On earth as it is in heaven.*
> *Give us this day our daily bread.*
> *And forgive us our debts,*
> *As we forgive our debtors.*
> *And do not lead us into temptation,*
> *But deliver us from the evil one.*
> *For Yours is the kingdom and the power and the glory forever. Amen.*

I remember reciting this prayer from the time I was probably six years of age until I was eighteen. I would say it once during our daily family devotions, then five days a week at school. I've calculated that in those years alone I recited it at least 8760 times.

But in those years of my youth, the words of the Lord's Prayer were mostly just memorized words. They were what I call head knowledge, but not something I really walked out in shoe leather every day. Getting these words from head to my heart definitely has been a journey. To be honest, it is still an ongoing daily journey for me. I am discovering that this prayer has so many layers of depth and truth. As a grandmother of nine grandchildren, I am still a work in progress.

Repeating the Lord's prayer like rosary prayer beads or any other repetitious prayer will not make us any more holy or spiritual; nor will it make God answer my prayers quicker. That's like trying to get on the good side of God. That's religion, not God's way. Thinking about it that way wears me out.

But the Lord's Prayer is a key prayer of the kingdom of God and we need to understand what that kingdom is all about.

The kingdom of God is the extension of God's rule and dominion in the earth and the universe. God calls us to be representatives or ambassadors of this kingdom even as we live our lives on earth. It's a daily journey from the minute you wake up in the morning and put your feet on the floor. This life is exciting, and filled with hope, peace, and joy that no one can take that away. Why? Because this kingdom comes from the heavenly realm. We represent and live God's character every day, all day long. You and I are the vessel, the conduit, the expression of Christ in us, the hope of glory.

This means we are a kind of alien, walking out Jesus' life on earth. Our real address is in the heavenly realm. We have been given the ability and grace to influence our community, our city, our state or province, our country for God's purposes. We are not of this world, although we are living in it.

As citizens in God's kingdom, we recognize His voice and we learn to recognize the counterfeit voices of lies. I was a cashier at one point in my working career. We were taught the real dollar bill so that the moment the counterfeit came along, we should know immediately it was a counterfeit bill.

The Word of God declares, *"My sheep hear my voice…and they follow me"* (John 10:27). Similarly, a baby in the womb hears her mother's voice and comes to recognize the vibrations and pitch of the mother's voice immediately. Before my children were born, I would spend time either singing or playing the piano. I would pray and also talk to them. I would speak blessing on them. All my children recognized my voice (they are also all musically inclined with a sense of rhythm and perfect pitch). In the same way, when you are attached to God and you spend much intimate time with the Lord, you will respond immediately to God's voice.

The kingdom of God is a present reality. The Scriptures say, "*The kingdom of God is within you*" (Luke 17:21). This is present tense which means that the kingdom is not for a future time. It is at hand or within reach.

The kingdom of God is more real than the kingdoms or governments of this world. Some of the earthly governments are democratic, meaning the people have the freedom to vote, and the majority government runs the country. Where there is a dictatorship, the people of the country must bow to the ruler. The people have no say. The kingdom of God is theocratic, which means that God rules. This means Jesus is King of Kings and Lord of Lords. You and I who are of the heavenly realm are attached to the king on His throne, who gives us the privilege to be His representatives and witnesses to the peoples of this earth. What an honour to have been given the authority to rule and reign with Jesus Christ not just in the future, but now!

God describes those who have been born again as a "royal priesthood" (1 Peter 2:9). We have been made kings and priests with the same authority that Jesus has. Do you get it? Do you see how honoured you are because of King Jesus?

ADDITIONAL READING: Mark 4:30–32; Mark 9:1; Mark 10:14–16; Mark 12:34; Mark 15:43–47; Luke 4:43; Luke 6:20; Luke 8:10; John 3:3–5; Acts 1:3; Acts 8:12; Acts 14:22; Acts 28:28–31; Romans 14:17–18; 1 Corinthians 4:20; 1 Corinthians 15:50; Hebrews 1:8; James 2:5; Revelation 12:10–11.

CHAPTER FIVE

Planting the Seed

JUST AS A SEED PLANTED IN THE GROUND GROWS INTO THE PLANT FROM WHICH it came, so God plants a seed in our spirit that offers us the full potential of growing into the image of Christ.

Jesus is the seed (John 1:1–4; 12:24; 1 Peter 1:23) who was planted in the earth that a harvest might come. This same seed is planted in you and me when we receive Jesus Christ into our heart through the Holy Spirit. The seed that has been planted in your spirit has the full potential of fully conforming us into Christ's image. That is why it says in God's Word that from glory to glory He is changing us. Paul says in Galatians 4:19, "*I labor in birth again until Christ is formed in you.*" Paul's heart for the Galatian church was that they would experience all the fullness of God in every measure. That is the heart of an apostle.

When we begin to understand the incredible seed of God placed into us, we will want to pursue Him.

Here is a very profound thought. God is not moved by need but by seed. Before the foundation of the world, God had a plan to restore His creation. He put a plan in place that would do just that:

Even as He chose us in Him before the foundation of the world, that we should be holy and without blemish before Him in love: having fore-ordained us unto adoption as sons through Jesus Christ unto himself, according to the good pleasure of His will.

—Ephesians 1:4–5 (ASV)

Here is a guarantee. God says in Isaiah 55:6–13:

Seek the LORD while He may be found, call upon Him while He is near. Let the wicked forsake his way, and the unrighteous man his thoughts; let him return to the LORD, and He will have mercy on him; and to our God, for He will abundantly pardon. "For My thoughts are not your thoughts, nor are your ways My ways," says the LORD. "For as the heavens are higher than the earth, so are My ways higher than your ways, and My thoughts than your thoughts.

For as the rain comes down, and the snow from heaven, and do not return there, but water the earth, and make it bring forth and bud, that it may give seed to the sower and bread to the eater, so shall My word be that goes forth from My mouth; it shall not return to Me void, but it shall accomplish what I please, and it shall prosper in the thing for which I sent it. For you shall go out with joy, and be led out with peace; the mountains and the hills shall break forth into singing before you, and all the trees of the field shall clap their hands. Instead of the thorn shall come up the cypress tree, and instead of the brier shall come up the myrtle tree; and it shall be to the LORD for a name, for an everlasting sign that shall not be cut off."

Isaiah wrote and prophesied this approximately seven hundred years before Jesus came onto the scene. God had this wonderful plan set in place before time. He spoke it in the realm of eternity where is no space or time. God has, throughout Scripture, continuously reminded mankind to trust Him. He is still saying this to you and me today.

When we trust in the Lord, we are saying that the kingdom of God is Christ–centred and not human–centred. All of a sudden, you are not thinking with the natural mind, but with the mind of Christ. Our desires become His desires. Our plans become His plans. Our perceived truth becomes God's truth. Our dream becomes God's dream. My will becomes His will. My emotions become His emotions. What is God passionate about? The kingdom of God is "*…righteousness and peace and joy in the Holy Spirit*" (Romans 14:17).

I grew up in a church where the pastors were focused on a human–centred mentality. We were always begging God to forgive us because if we didn't, God would smite us or we could lose our salvation. The emphasis was on us and working up a froth of "woe is me, I'm such a sinner." They emphasized fear rather than faith. Preaching was controlling so we could be held in tow. Religion does that: please run from that thinking as fast as you can. To remain only keeps you in religious bondage.

As a new (or perhaps even an older) Christ–follower, you need to understand the church is not a brick–and–mortar building but a body of believers. We are the building, the temple which is the incarnation or expression of God in the earth.

Mary the virgin was impregnated by the Holy Spirit. Jesus grew in her and she gave birth to Jesus, who is also called Emmanuel, which means God with us. Now the seed that impregnated us through the Holy Spirit caused us to become alive or be born again, which makes us the ongoing Christ in the earth. What an honour, place and position we have been called to. We have God's DNA and we live our life out of Him. It is a humbling thought but it is true.

In Luke 9:57–62, Jesus taught about discipleship. He tells us there is a cost to discipleship and offers us the choice to set our priorities with God or not. To one man He said, "*Let the dead bury their own dead, but you go and preach the kingdom of God*" (Luke 9:60). Another man said, "*I will follow you but let me first go bid them farewell who are at my house*" (Luke 9:61). Jesus said to him, "*No one, having put his hand to the plow, and looking back, is fit for the kingdom of God*" (Luke 9:62). This is a call for full commitment.

Jesus uses the image of the harvest to teach us what He calls us to. In Matthew 9:37–38, He says, "*The harvest truly is plentiful, but the laborers are few. Therefore pray the Lord of the harvest to send out laborers into His harvest.*" The same story is told in Luke 10.

That is the clarion call for all who believe: to be harvesters. Using different images, Jesus says, "*Follow me, and I will make you fishers of men*" (Matthew 4:19).

The Word of God tells us we have all the tools we need to bring in the harvest. First, we have Holy Spirit to give us God's power, and to lead, guide, and teach us all things. Jesus says we have been given all wisdom, for if we lack wisdom, He will give it to us. He covers us with His protection. He encamps around about them that fear Him. We have the power of the Holy Spirit to cast out demons in Jesus' name. We can raise the dead through the resurrection power that dwells in us. When we speak and declare healing in Jesus' name, the work has already been completed through the cross of Jesus Christ.

We have nothing to fear, because Jesus is our peace. He is our rest. He is our joy. He is our righteousness. We, His children, are partakers of it all. We are equipped and are fully persuaded that what God has promised, He will do, so others too might have the opportunity to believe on Jesus Christ the Son of God.

As those who bear the seed of the Lord and who are harvesters, we can know that we are covered by the Lord. God is faithful.

ADDITIONAL READING: Philippians 3:14; Galatians 4:19; Galatians 2:20.

CHAPTER SIX
The Planting of the Seed

I WAS HONOURED TO BE RAISED IN A WONDERFUL CHRISTIAN HOME. BOTH OUR parents loved the Lord Jesus Christ, and so my four siblings and I learned much about the importance of Bible reading and prayer, and how we were to walk it out in our daily lives. We grew up recognizing similarities in character and personality and looks. We knew without a shadow of doubt we all looked somewhat like Dad or Mom. At the same time, we were each unique. We had the DNA of our parents, but we also each had our own unique fingerprint.

So it is when you are born again: God's DNA is implanted into your spirit. You come alive. You are a new creation. I believe this is one of the most important subjects any person on this earth needs to know as a believer and follower of Jesus Christ. It is really important for the person who is still in the valley of decision about choosing to follow Jesus Christ. This revelation is a life–changer.

We have talked about how God plants his seed in your spirit, how Jesus Christ begins to grow in you as you are watered and fed on the Living Word of God. In many ways this process is similar to growing a garden. As an avid gardener for many years, I love to watch a seed I've planted and watered begin to sprout. With more watering and lots of sun, and pulling of weeds, these tomato plants (or other crops) finally bear fully mature fruit. What a joy it is to see and taste the crop when it's time for harvesting.

Let's look at what God plants in us. God plants His divine nature in us. This seed gets watered with His Word, germinates and grows until we become a full-grown, mature person with the nature of Christ. Just as a vegetable grows from seed to full maturity, we too experience stages of growth. Here are some Scriptures that open up the powerful mystery of Christ in you:

By which have been given to us exceedingly great and precious promises, that through these you may be partakers of the divine nature, having escaped the corruption that is in the world through lust. But also for this very reason, giving all diligence, add to your faith virtue, to virtue knowledge, to knowledge self-control, to self-control perseverance, to perseverance godliness, to godliness brotherly kindness, and to brotherly kindness love. For if these things are yours and abound, you will be neither barren nor unfruitful in the knowledge of our Lord Jesus Christ.
—2 Peter 1:4–8

The Amplified Version of the same passage says,

For by these He has bestowed on us His precious and magnificent promises [of inexpressible value], so that by them you may escape from the immoral freedom that is in the world because of disreputable desire, and become sharers of the divine nature. For this very reason, applying your diligence [to the divine promises, make every effort] in [exercising] your faith to, develop moral excellence, and in moral excellence, knowledge (insight, understanding), and in your knowledge, self-control, and in your self-control, steadfastness, and in your steadfastness, godliness, and in your godliness, brotherly affection, and in your brotherly affection, [develop Christian] love [that is, learn to unselfishly seek the best for others and to do things for their benefit]. For as these qualities are yours and are increasing [in you as you grow toward spiritual maturity], they will keep you from being useless and unproductive in regard to the true knowledge and greater understanding of our Lord Jesus Christ.
—2 Peter 1:4–8 (AMP)

"As God has said: I will dwell in them and walk among them. I will be their God, and they shall be my people."

—2 Corinthians 6:16

God plants this seed in our heart and spirit. So we respond by letting His faith arise, and believing for our healing and for the baptism of the Holy Spirit that we might walk in divine health, resurrection life and so much more. With the faith of Jesus, we embrace His nature and His character, and lay hold and embrace His grace, the enabling power of God.

We can know that just as we harvest fruit that grows from seeds, so there will be a harvest of the seed that is planted in us.

CHAPTER SEVEN
Adding to Faith

MOST CHRISTIANS JUST WANT A GOOD REPORT CARD. WE WANT "A GOOD testimony" is said of us, as God said of the elders in Hebrews 12:1–2. But I submit to you that in Jesus we can have the promise of a better thing through a better covenant. And what is that better thing that God has promised? It is the faith of Jesus. He's the one who authored and who will finish our faith. Our kingdom walk does not rest on our faith but on His faith, the faith of God.

As the Apostle Paul wrote:

I have been crucified with Christ; it is no longer I who live, but Christ lives in me; and the life which I now live in the flesh, I live by the faith of the Son of God, who loved me and gave himself for me.
—Galatians 2:20

Hebrews 11:3 tells us, "*By faith we understand that the worlds were framed by the word of God, so that the things which are seen were not made of things which are visible.*" In Romans 12:3, we read:

For I say, through the grace given to me, to everyone who is among you, not to think of himself more highly than he ought to think, but to think soberly, as God has dealt to each one a measure of faith.

The faith of Jesus works by His love. His love believes all things according to 1 Corinthians 13:1-13. This faith is certain, sure, and supports all things found in Jesus Christ. It is the faith through which He framed the world.

We need to understand that we are moving from elementary faith to mature faith, His faith. Jesus' faith conquered death and obtained the promise of God. That kind and quality of faith are in the heart of every believer.

How is it that we move from an elementary to a mature faith? In 2 Peter 1:5–6, God explains that we need to add various elements to our faith. He explains what these are:

"But also for this very reason, giving all diligence, add to your faith virtue, to virtue knowledge, to knowledge self-control, to self-control perseverance, to perseverance godliness, to godliness brotherly kindness, and to brotherly kindness love."

Let's break these down.

ADD TO YOUR FAITH VIRTUE

Strong's Concordance tells us that virtue means: one of excellence, a force, an army, wealth, virtue, valor, strength, band of men, host, might, power, riches, substance, train, valiantly, war, worthy.

Webster's Dictionary says: someone who is virtuous is blameless, equitable, exemplary, excellent, good, honest, moral, noble, righteous, upright, worthy, chaste, continent, immaculate, innocent, modest, pure, undefiled, efficacious, powerful.

Have you ever heard the statement, "She (or he) is a force to be reckoned with?" From an earthly mindset, this perception might describe someone who would intimidate you. But God gives an example of a different force to be reckoned with, a force of light and power. In Proverbs 31, God describes the virtuous woman as one who excels in excellence and integrity, someone who demonstrates the ability to run businesses, someone who embraces truth, nobility, justice, purity, love, and someone of excellent report. This virtuous person is not someone who stresses and strains and works really hard at completing this list of qualities, but instead is virtuous when they received the inheritance of Jesus Christ. As you and I yield to the Lordship of Jesus, those qualities will flow out of us. For God is a God of virtue. The battle has been won.

ADDITIONAL READING: Matthew, 5:30; Luke 6:19; Luke 8:46; 2 Peter 1:3,5; Ruth 3:11; Proverbs 12:4 Proverbs 31:10; Proverbs 31:29, Philippians 4:8

TO VIRTUE [ADD] KNOWLEDGE

In Hosea 4:6, God says, "*My people are destroyed for lack of knowledge.*" In fact, as the glory of God shines brighter and brighter through His people, the knowledge of God will be seen and understood, even as His divine revelation is being expressed.

Listen to what God says about knowledge:

Now thanks be to God who always leads us in triumph in Christ, and through us diffuses the fragrance of His knowledge in every place.
—2 Corinthians 2:14

For it is the God who commanded light to shine out of darkness, who has shone in our hearts to give the light of the knowledge of the glory of God in the face of Jesus Christ.
—2 Corinthians 4:6

But as you abound in everything—in faith, in speech, in knowledge, in all diligence, and in your love for us—see that you abound in this grace also.
—2 Corinthians 8:7

That the God of our Lord Jesus Christ, the Father of glory, may give to you the spirit of wisdom and revelation in the knowledge of Him....
—Ephesians 1:17

But as it is written: Eye has not seen, nor ear heard, nor have entered into the heart of man the things which God has prepared for those who love Him.

—1 Corinthians 2: 9

For this cause I, Paul, the prisoner of Jesus Christ for you Gentiles—if indeed you have heard of the dispensation of the grace of God which was given me to for you: how that by revelation he made known to me the mystery…by which, when you read, you may understand my knowledge in the mystery of Christ.

—Ephesians 3:1–4

Then in verse nineteen, *"to know the love of Christ which passes knowledge; that you might be filled with all the fullness of God"* (Ephesians 3:19). This verse is particularly special to me because as a teenager, I was reading the Word when that verse popped off the pages of my Bible. I knew if that was possible, I desired it. I want to experience the fullness of God in my lifetime. Even now as I write about it years later, I am daily realizing the knowledge of the greatness and awesomeness of the length and depth and height of God's love.

As I look back over this time, I'm also amazed at the increase in knowledge in our world. Much is very good, although knowledge can be used in a negative way. I think of technology: as I have watched transitions in media and computer technology, I can see both ways in which our world has deteriorated and ways in which this knowledge can be used for good. I believe God is smiling when obedient, Spirit–led vessels use media to share the knowledge and witness of the gospel of Jesus Christ. Currently, I am part of a church ministry that offers an online streaming church ministry and training centre that is impacting people in many parts of the world. I am honoured to be part of this Body of believers who accept you as part of the family whether you are physically present or not. I currently live two hours away from the church, and so don't always make it in person to the service. The fact that knowledge can increase through computer technology has been an answer to my heart's cry. The Word of God is coming quickly! The enemy has been using technology for his strategic plan, but God is over–riding Satan's plan, as the Body of Christ uses technology and other modes to bring in this end–time harvest that God has planned and envisioned.

ADDITIONAL READING: Ephesians 4:13; Philippians 1:9; Philippians 3:8; Colossians1:9–10; Colossians 2:3; Colossians 3:10; 1 Timothy 2:4; 2 Timothy 3:7; Hebrews 10:26; James 3: 13; 1 Peter 3:7; 2 Peter 1: 2,3,5,6,8.; 2 Peter 2:20; 2 Peter 3:18.

TO KNOWLEDGE [ADD] SELF–CONTROL

While Jesus was on earth and was about His Father's business, He only spoke what the Father told Him to say. His words were profound, concise, and self–controlled. He exercised restraint when He walked into the temple. He demonstrated self–control as He saw the people buying and selling their stuff.

Using intimidation through yelling or screaming at someone is not the heart of God. That comes out of a spirit of fear and control. You speak out of the well of God's divine nature when using self–control. That is why Jesus often went to a quiet place to meet and commune with heavenly Father. He is our example.

Galatians 5: 22–25 tells us:

But the fruit of the Spirit is love, joy, peace, long suffering, kindness, goodness, faithfulness, gentleness, self–control. Against such there is no law. And those who are Christ's have crucified the flesh with its passions and desires. If we live in the Spirit, let us also walk in the Spirit.

What is the opposite of self–control? The dictionary tells us that if we lack self–control we are defiant, disorderly, headstrong, inconsistent, insubordinate, mischievous, naughty, non–compliant, ungoverned, unrestrained, unruly, untrained, and wayward. Take your own temperature. If these are words that still describe you or me, then recognize that a mindset change is necessary. Perhaps you are not yet aware that you have been seated with Jesus on His throne, and given all authority and power to break any of those things in your life. You embrace the mind of Christ who is self–controlled in everyday life. We are overcomers in Christ by submitting to what is already yours and mine. It is our inheritance. It is a journey and is progressive. God loves you and me so much that He offers us His great and unending love, and tells us to go and sin no more.

ADDITIONAL READING: 2 Peter 1: 1–11; Revelation 12:10–12; Proverbs 18:21.

TO SELF–CONTROL [ADD] PERSEVERANCE

James 1:2–4 counsels believers, saying:

> *My brethren, count it all joy when you fall into various trials, knowing that the testing of your faith produces patience. But let patience have its perfect work, that you may be perfect and complete, lacking nothing.*

Perseverance means to be patient, to endure, suffer, and abide. It means we embrace something, grab hold of it and not let it go. So let's allow patience be perfected in you and me.

Remember, I mentioned earlier that we grow like plants? I say, keep pressing in. Don't stop now. When that part of God's divine seed comes forth bearing the fruit of patience, you will know that you have overcome by the word of your testimony and the blood of the Lamb. That's God's patience. Those tests will bring a testimony of the faithfulness of God who is full of patience. We can exchange our lack of patience which He already nailed to the Cross, and embrace His perfect patience until Christ is fully formed in us. After some time, we will recognize we have embraced the patience of Jesus. That seed that was planted in your spirit is beginning to blossom and before you know it, the fruit of patience will manifest through the sons of God as He intended. The world around us will see this manifestation of God's heart, and others will begin to embrace this life.

I have had many occasions over the years to respond out of the divine nature of Christ rather than out of impatience. For example, one time when I was driving in slow traffic, I felt impatience rising up. I thought, "What are they doing? I have no time to waste! I have things to do." Before I knew it, I was talking to the driver in front of me, raising my voice, and telling him, "Get moving buddy!" (he couldn't hear me, of course, but I was just talking out of complete frustration.) Suddenly, after fifty–plus years of driving, I realized this wasn't working, that something had to change. I said, "Lord! I do not want to be this way. Help me." I waited for God to speak, and finally I heard a still small voice say, "Olivia, enjoy the ride."

There came a grace (the enabling power of God, His divine influence) that rose up inside of me. Every time a situation came up, I cried out for more of God's grace. Finally, when I recognized I'm seated with Christ in heavenly places, I welcomed the soft quiet voice of Holy Spirit. "Enjoy the ride." Did this fruit of long-suffering or patience come on the tree and ripen immediately? Of course not. It was and is a journey. But I became aware each time I got in my car that this would be another opportunity to overcome through Christ.

Let's not shy away from trials or tests. I remember, I said to the Lord one day, "I really can't take any more—please help." There was a time where I felt I would literally die if the Lord would not intervene. God was gracious, and He poured in the oil and healing came into my life. I literally could see in the spirit realm how the enemy was being pushed back, as the angels came to surround me. I was weary. As I look back now, I was made aware I was trying to handle the situation in my own strength. If you or I are living the life of faith in our own strength, we will wear ourselves out and live in a state of frustration. It does not work. I was fretting and fuming and crying when I heard Him say, "Embrace my grace, and I will be your defence department." Finally I got the message. "Stop trying to do something in your own strength; be patient; I will work it out for you." He did.

So embrace the patience of Christ. After all, you have God's DNA. It is the enabling power of God and His covenant to you and me to actually be able to say, "I count it all joy when I fall into various trials, knowing the testing of my faith produces patience."

ADDITIONAL READING: Roman 5: 3–4; 1 Timothy 6: 11; Romans 8: 18–25 (note verse twenty-five); 2 Timothy 3: 10–17 (note verse ten); Romans 15: 4–10; Hebrews 6: 9–12; Colossians 1:9–18 (note verse eleven); Hebrews 12: 1–2; 1 Thessalonians 1: 2–5; James 1: 3–4; 2 Thessalonians 1:4; Revelation 1:9.

TO PATIENCE [ADD] GODLINESS

My parents had a love for the Lord, there was no doubt about it, but their understanding stemmed from a religious tradition which expressed itself in fear. It was more like a condemning fear. For them, that was their understanding and reality. To them, this was walking in godliness.

Growing up under this influence, I walked under much fear, fearful I would lose my salvation if I did anything that did not line up with their rules. For example, I could not wear lipstick or jewelry, go to dances, drink, smoke or do drugs. Going to movies was a big "no–no." One time when I was about sixteen, I wanted so much to go to a movie that came into town—"The Ten Commandments." I snuck out of the house and found my way to the theatre. I justified myself that it was going to be a movie about a Bible story, so what was so wrong about that? I paid to get in, sat down and began watching the movie. I was mesmerized by the big screen. After about fifteen or twenty minutes, though, my conscience bothered me so much that I walked out. I was afraid to go home, but I did, and faced the wrath of my parents.

The religious rules and regulations brought a lot of confusion for me. But I was sure that if I followed the rules this made me more holy and godly and more acceptable to God. You see it was all about outward appearance, but in my heart I knew I was rebelling. Why couldn't I go to my high school prom? Of course, there would be dancing. If I went, I would not be godly.

When I finished high school and moved to the big city, you can bet the big world out there slapped me upside the face with temptations galore. When I got out of the cage of rules and regulations, and was on my own, I went a bit nuts and checked a few things out, although always under the cloud of condemnation.

Satan thought he had me in the palm of his hand but the Holy Spirit was continually drawing me so I could experience the Father's love. He just would not let me go. Deep down inside, I knew He loved me and He had His hand on my life. I realized one day I was at a crossroads. I cried out of the desperation of my heart, "Please, help me Lord! I truly want you more than anything in all the world." I realized, I hadn't lost my salvation, but that God was looking for that deeper and personal relationship with Him.

The truth is that godliness does not come from rules or regulation, but from an intimate relationship with the Lord.

It took a number of years, but I knew that if I was willing to seek first the kingdom of God and His righteousness, all of God's love would be added to me. As the religious rules started dropping off and I realized I was hiding with Christ in God, I no longer felt condemned. As I experienced the robe of righteousness placed on me, Jesus' robe of righteousness, my desires began to change. I yielded to my Lord, recognizing that any holiness, any godliness came from embracing Jesus Christ, the Head over me. As I desired to spend time with the Lord, I wanted to read the Bible; I wanted to commune with the Lord; I desired only to please Him. My heart and mindset began to change. I recognized His grace and power to resist those temptations more and more. I am holy, because Jesus is holy, and He made it possible through His obedience to go to the cross and shed that perfect sinless blood. He was buried, He arose from the grave and now He is ascended and seated on the throne. It is finished! Then when I found out I was seated with Him as part of the Body, a whole new understanding and revelation was opened to me. I see the great divide between man–made religious thinking and intimate relationship with my Lord. It was totally opposite; works versus grace.

The more I pressed into Him and embraced Him, I recognized it's all about Him. There came a reverence for God, a desire to worship Him, because it is all about Him. My old life is gone and buried: I am risen with Christ, and seated with Him.

As you embrace God's divine nature, there comes a deep longing to worship and reverence God's presence. It is placed in the forefront of anything in life. As you begin to know and experience the holiness of

God, there is nothing else you'd rather be doing. The sense of honour enlarges and increases as you spend more and more time with your Lord Jesus Christ. As the old chorus goes, "Turn your eyes upon Jesus, look full in His wonderful face. And the things of earth will grow strangely dim, in the light of His glory and grace."

Godliness will just flow out of you. Whatever you do or say is expressed from a heart of worship and adoration to your King Jesus. It's a heart condition. Godliness is within that seed that was planted in the womb of your spirit. That's who you are because that's who Jesus is. The Body expresses the kingdom, the divine nature of God in the earth, till the whole earth is filled with His glory.

ADDITIONAL READING: Galatians 4:19; 2 Peter 1:2–4.

TO GODLINESS [ADD] BROTHERLY KINDNESS

It is in God's divine nature to show divine kindness. The world may show acts of kindness, but is it possible they are looking for a self–motivated return for their acts of kindness? So then, how is God's kindness different?

Even through the forty years the Israelites journeyed in the wilderness, God demonstrated so much patience towards them, when they complained, when they became proud and hardened their heart, and even when they were in defiant rebellion against God. Finally, God let them wallow in their sin as the enemy took them over. I am sure that deeply hurt the heart of God, but they were making a choice. They deliberately came out and away from God's blessing.

Brotherly kindness means fraternal affection. This kindness is expressed by extending honour and respect for one another. Brothers and sisters stick together, back up and support one another. That is expressing kindness. This kindness prefers one another, and places that other person before them. The brilliance of God's glory will begin to shine more and more throughout and within the church community as we practice brotherly kindness. When the world sees such kindness in action, they will be amazed. Their curiosity will get the best of them, and they will want to check it out. They are responding to the divine nature of God—His kindness.

Psalm 117:1–2 says:

Praise the LORD, all you Gentiles!
Laud Him, all you peoples!
For His merciful kindness is great toward us,
And the truth of the LORD endures forever.
Praise the LORD!

The Proverbs 31 woman we talked about before is described as follows: "*She opens her mouth with wisdom; and on her tongue is the law of kindness*" (Proverbs 31:26). In the Bible, men are also called to brotherly kindness. If you will dig deeper you can liken this chapter to the Bride of Christ where there is neither male nor female: this virtue of brotherly kindness belongs to all who are partakers of God's divine nature.

Paul, in 2 Corinthians: 6, shares his life of suffering and his care for the Corinthian church. In verse six, he is expressing his love through brotherly kindness. Remember, when expressing this brotherly kindness, Paul is showing an example of being an influencer of kindness according to Christ's example. This is powerful and becomes an act of worship and honour to God.

ADDITIONAL READING: Colossians 3:12 –17; Titus 3:1–7; 2 Peter 1:3–11; Isaiah 54:1–17 (note verses 8 and 10).

TO BROTHERLY KINDNESS [ADD] LOVE

One morning, I had a vision of the Father's love. It was still dark outside and I was in bed, when out of me came words in an unknown language: I was speaking in tongues. I knew I was in the Spirit and I was speaking words of adoration and worship to God. After a couple of minutes, a melody in tongues flowed out of my mouth. During those moments, I felt my spirit move to a place somewhere in the heavenly realm, away from my bedroom. I began to experience this intense atmosphere of love around me, and then it penetrated right through me. It was like being totally immersed, as if I had jumped into a pool of water. I could sense this love was pure beyond anything I had experienced in the earthly realm. I was transfixed by this love. I knew then that this was the love of the Father. I wanted to stay and never come back, but I knew there had to be a purpose for what I was experiencing. I needed to share this kind of love and compassion with others. It was the love the Father has for all peoples of the earth.

I remembered a Scripture my pastor had explained when I was a teenager. It really stayed and resonated with me: Ephesians 3:19 says, *"to know the love of Christ which passes knowledge; that you may be filled with all the fullness of God."*

I found myself raising my arms up, and singing in a language of love to Father God. I heard Him say to me, "This kind of love caused me to send Jesus to the earth."

In my vision, others were there too. In this worship time, I was made aware of us being knit together as one in Christ. We all were in Him and He was in us and we were all in the Father. This perfect oneness was God's plan before the foundation of the world. It was like a spiritual building whose builder and maker is God, and I was part of this building with others where we were fitly joined together to make this beautiful dwelling place where Jesus resided. It is like the Scripture that says that a husband and his wife become one flesh. We are one building, and it was perfect, and the foundation was upon Jesus Christ. I recognized there was no prejudice in this vision because we were overcome by this intense love of God. I could not see any difference in colour or culture. Prejudice was not in our vocabulary. We were all equal in the Spirit.

When I finally came back to an awareness of being in bed, it seemed like only a few moments had passed, but to my surprise it had been two-and-a-half hours. I noticed an intense weightiness of God's presence. The blanket covering me seemed very heavy, and I could not move. It was at this moment I had this intense desire to just worship in my spirit, as the tears flowed down my cheeks and onto my pillow. I knew I had been profoundly changed. Suddenly I was looking through a different spiritual lens. I knew any opinions I might have had did not matter. They were not significant in the light of what I had just experienced. My journeys in life were stepping stones to get me to this profound place in Him. I knew this was not just for me, but for all who will enter in, and move forward by pressing into the prize of the high calling in Christ Jesus.

Listen to what God says to us in Jeremiah 31:3–4:

Yes, I have loved you with an everlasting love; therefore, with loving-kindness I have drawn you. Again I will build you and you shall be rebuilt, O virgin of Israel! You shall again be adorned with your tambourines, and shall go forth in the dances of those who rejoice.

Listen too to Romans 8:37–39:

Yet in all these things we are more than conquerors through Him who loved us. For I am persuaded that neither death nor life, nor angels nor principalities nor powers, nor things present nor things to come, nor height nor depth, nor any other created thing shall be able to separate us from the love of God which is in Christ Jesus our Lord.

When we grow into our mature faith in Christ, love is the highest point.

ADDITIONAL READING: John 3:16; Ephesians 2: 4–10; 2 Thessalonians 2: 16–17; Mark 12:30; 1 Corinthians 2: 9; 1 Corinthians 8: 3–6; Galatians 2:20; 2 Thessalonians 1: 3–5; Hebrews 6: 10–12; James 1:12; 1 John 2:5–6; 1 John 3:10–23; 1 John 4:7–11.

CHAPTER EIGHT

What is the Kingdom?

ROMANS 14:17 SAYS, "*FOR THE KINGDOM OF GOD IS...RIGHTEOUSNESS AND peace and joy in the Holy Spirit.*" Let's take a quick look at what this looks like.

RIGHTEOUSNESS

Strong's concordance tells us righteousness means innocent, holy, justified. The blood of Jesus is so powerful that all our sins have been dealt with through the perfect Lamb of God.

Romans 3:21–22 tells us:

> *But now the righteousness of God apart from the law is revealed, being witnessed by the law and the prophets, even the righteousness of God, through faith in Jesus Christ, to all and on all who believe.*

Matthew 3:15 says, "*But Jesus answered and said to him, 'Permit it to be so now, for thus it is fitting for us to fulfill all righteousness.' Then he allowed Him.*"

ADDITIONAL READING: Matthew 3: 6–17; Matthew 5:6, 17–20; Matthew 21:28–32; John 16:5–15; Acts 10: 34–43; Acts 13: 9–10; Romans 1:16–17; Romans (chapters 3–14); Ephesians 4:24, 5:9,6:14; Philippians 1:11; Philippians 3:6,9; 1 Timothy 6:11; 2 Timothy chapters 2–4; Titus 3:5; Hebrews 1:8–9; 5:13; 7:2;11:7, 13; 12:11; James 1:20; 2:23; 3:18; 1 Peter

2:24; 2 Peter 1:1; 2:5,21; 3:13; 1 John 2:29; 3:7, 10; Revelation 19:8,11.

PEACE

The Hebrew word shalom is translated as peace. It means safety, health, prosperity, favour, friendship, rest, and well being.

Psalm 85:8–10 says:

I will hear what God the Lord will speak, for He will speak peace to His people and to His saints; But let them not turn back to folly. Surely His salvation is near to those who fear Him, that glory may dwell in our land. Mercy and truth have met together; righteousness and peace have kissed.

John 14:27 says:

Peace I leave with you, my peace I give to you; not as the world gives do I give to you. Let not your heart be troubled, neither let it be afraid.

ADDITIONAL READING: Acts 10:36; Romans 5:1; Romans 8:6; Romans 14:17–19; Romans 16:20; 1 Corinthians 14:33; Galatians 5:22; Ephesians 2:14; Philippians 4:7–15; Colossians 3:15; Hebrews 12:14; James 3:18; Matthew 5:9.

JOY

Joy originates from knowing Jesus and His immovable and everlasting kingdom. It is the spiritual substance and the tangible response to the never–ending truth, knowledge and revelation of Jesus Christ and His kingdom.

This joy cannot be conjured up in your own strength. You and I have no strength; we have God's strength and power dwelling in us. We embrace Joy, who is God. We walk it out with this abiding and knowing presence of God that is joy. This is not necessarily the kind that causes us to want to do cartwheels all the time, but a joy that radiates out of us with the knowledge and revelation of that which characterizes God through Jesus Christ, manifested through Holy Spirit in us. When I get together with another child of God with the mind of Christ, from deep in my spirit there arises an intense desire to want to share the goodness of God, which in turn provides this joy of knowing Christ in you, the hope of glory. It can express itself in dancing, laughter, tears of joy or shouts of praise. All I know is that, for me, the resource of joy is an eternal and everlasting well that never will run dry. If you attach joy to a natural emotion, you will be disappointed, because feelings are deceptive. One day you will be flying high with happy, happy feelings, and then the next day you'll be down in the dumps. This is not consistent with the Word of God and the character or divine nature of God. So let's embrace God's joy.

ADDITIONAL READING: Luke 15:7; Matthew 2:10; Luke 10:17–20; John 3:27–30; John 15:1–11; John 16:16–20; Acts 13: 44–52; Acts 15:3–4; Acts 20: 18–31; Galatians 5:22; Philippians 2:2–4; Hebrews 2:2 James 1:2; 1 Peter 1: 6–9; 1 Peter 4:13; 1 John 1: 1–4; 3 John 1:4; Jude 1:24–25.

CHAPTER NINE

Living Out of God's Nature

IF WE WANT TO LIVE IN THE KINGDOM OF GOD, AS I HAVE SAID, WE CANNOT DO so out of our own strength; we must do so by living out of the nature of God. I want us to look at several important characteristics of God's nature.

HIS FAITHFULNESS

God is faithful. This means he is permanent, true and certain, stable and trustworthy. God said to Israel, in Deuteronomy 7:9:

> *Therefore know that the Lord your God, He is God, the faithful God who keeps covenant and mercy for a thousand generations with those who love Him and keep His commandments.*

For too many, faithfulness is a foreign concept. But the faithfulness of God is eternal; the well will never run dry. God's faithfulness is who God is. He won't rip you off like perhaps a friend has. God, will never let you down. God is a good God. He won't dump you if you don't toe the line. Never! His love is unconditional. Now that's a winning combination. Even if you are unfaithful to the Lord, He can't stop loving you. He is faithful.

Why can I say this? You and I who have received this free gift of salvation, are attached to the Head which is Jesus, the truth and the life. He's your protector and help in time of need. He is everything you've ever hoped for. He is faithful.

Listen to what the Scriptures say about God's faithfulness:

*Your mercy, O Lord, is in the heavens; Your faithfulness reaches to the
clouds.*

—Psalm 36:5

*Trust in the Lord, and do good; dwell in the land, and feed on His
faithfulness. Delight yourself also in the Lord, and He shall give you the
desires of your heart.*

—Psalm 37: 3–4

*His lord said to him, "Well done, good and faithful servant; you have
been faithful over a few things, I will make you ruler over many things.
Enter into the joy of your lord."*

—Matthew 25:23

*God is faithful, by whom you were called into the fellowship of His Son,
Jesus Christ our Lord.*

—1 Corinthians 1:9

*No temptation has overtaken you except such as is common to man; but
God is faithful who will not allow you to be tempted beyond what you
are able, but with the temptation will also make the way of escape, that
you may be able to bear it.*

—1 Corinthians 10:13

ADDITIONAL READING: Lamentations 3:20–24; Psalms 71:1–24;
Psalm 89:1–52; Psalm 92:1–15; Psalm 105:1–45; Psalm
111:1–16; Isaiah 11:1–16; Isaiah 25:1; Romans 3:2–3; Galatians 5:22–25.

HIS GENTLENESS

In 2 Samuel 22:1–51, David had just been delivered from his enemies.
His experience was one you wouldn't wish on anyone but he responded

by declaring the awesomeness of God in the form of a song of praise. What caught my ear in that song was in verse thirty-six where he sang, "*Your gentleness has made me great.*" Whatever David had to go through, I am aware God did not browbeat him with harshness of words; neither did He push or prod him. There was a tone, an attitude in His voice that David responded to. You may know a few people like that.

I know, having raised three children and a number of foster children, as well as helping my daughter with her two girls as she went to college, that the key to success was speaking to them with gentleness. Did I always succeed? No, of course not, but for the most part I was able to overcome with the help and grace of God. As a foster parent, there were some strict guidelines we needed to follow: raising your voice was not conducive to their needs. They already felt rejected and abandoned; they needed love. I had many opportunities to be a shower of gentleness and kindness. Kids just need to know they are loved, even when they make poor choices.

My parents both exhibited the spirit of gentleness. As their children, we were totally blessed. There were rules, and we learned to follow the rules. If we chose not to, of course they would follow through with discipline. Things seemed very clear to me: don't cross that line again. But, they always did it with gentleness.

The apostle Paul exhibited the attribute of gentleness toward the Thessalonian church: "*But we were gentle among you, just as a nursing mother cherishes her own children*" (1 Thessalonians 2: 7).

God commends gentleness:

And a servant of the Lord must not quarrel but be gentle to all, able to teach, patient, in humility correcting those who are in opposition, if God perhaps will grant them repentance so that they may know the truth, and that they may come to their senses and escape the snare of the devil, having been taken captive by him to do his will.
—2 Timothy 2:24–26

Remind them to be subject to rulers and authorities, to obey, to be ready for every good work, to speak evil of no one, to be peaceable, gentle, showing all humility to all men.

—Titus 3:1–2

But the wisdom that is from above is first pure, then peaceable, gentle, willing to yield, full of mercy and good fruits, without partiality and without hypocrisy.

—James 3:17

When sharing with others the gospel of Jesus Christ, being too aggressive is not the divine nature of Jesus; rather share with the spirit of gentleness, just like Jesus. That is his heart, and so is it ours moving forward.

ADDITIONAL READING: 1 Peter 2:18; Psalm 18:35; Isaiah 40:11; 2 Corinthians 10:1, 2–6; Galatians 5:22.

HIS COMPASSION

Awhile back, I was having a talk with the Lord and asking Him about compassion, compassion for the lost. I said to Him, "To be honest with you, Lord, I've been too busy working in church. I am doing a whole lot of stuff. There is something wrong because I sure don't feel like I have the compassion I should for those still lost and without You, Lord."

You see, that's what that "religion" does to a person. I justified myself that I was playing the piano, leading praise and worship, teaching a Bible class, involved in prayer group, cleaning toilets and vacuuming, doing Bible studies, and you name it, I was doing it. But the very thing that was missing in this equation was the fact people were going to hell. Maybe I was encouraging the believers, but where was my heart for the lost?

I decided to pray to ask Him to put compassion in my heart for those still needing to embrace Him.

One morning soon afterwards, I had a vision in which I felt compassion and love from Father God. This love opened my innermost part of my heart to see the lost, how God loved them just as He loves me. When I came out of this vision, I knew I was changed forever.

This end–time harvest is upon us and I know things were going to start changing for me. I began to weep from deep inside my spirit. My spiritual eyes were now looking through the filter of the Father's heart of compassion. When I pray now, my heart is intense with compassion. Grace embraced me and influenced my heart for change. This was quite new because frankly, I really had lost the Father God's heart for the lost. I had been churched with a religious mindset, and it was thick and crusty.

I know what it means to carry babies to full term and through to delivery. I experienced the love only a mother could know for the baby inside of me. It is indescribable. The compassion used to overwhelm me at times. I offered many prayers for each child during my pregnancies. But this doesn't begin to compare with the compassion of intercession that Jesus is doing right now for all of us here on earth, cries with a depth that I cannot describe. All I know is that God's love is so deep and high and wide—it's eternal. After all, Jesus paid the price already, it's finished, and He sits to make intercession for all.

There are stories of Jesus' compassion while He was on earth:

But when He saw the multitudes, He was moved with compassion for them, because they were weary and scattered, like sheep having no shepherd. Then He said to His disciples, "The harvest truly is plentiful, but the laborers are few. Therefore, pray the Lord of the harvest to send out laborers into His harvest."

—Matthew 9:36–38

And when Jesus went out He saw a great multitude; and He was moved with compassion for them, and healed their sick.

—Matthew 14:14

Another time, Jesus was teaching and He commanded His disciples to feed the crowds who were listening. Why did he do it? The Bible tells us Jesus said:

"I have compassion on the multitude, because they have now continued with Me three days and have nothing to eat. And I do not want to send them away hungry, lest they faint on the way."

—Matthew 15:32

He didn't ask a bunch of questions. He was just moved by the compassion that Father God has, and the people benefited by His acts of kindness.

When Peter asked Jesus how many times he should forgive his brother, Jesus answered with a parable (Matthew 18:21–35) of a king who forgave his servant's debt because he was moved with compassion—only to have the servant respond without compassion to someone who owed him money. It's good to pay it forward. It's always a heart issue.

In Matthew 20: 32–34, we see two blind men cry out for Jesus to have mercy and heal them. The Scripture tells us that Jesus had compassion and touched their eyes. And immediately their eyes received sight, and they followed Him.

Do you have difficulties expressing this kind of compassion? I submit to you that this is a key in the end–time harvest that's upon us.

Let's pray this prayer together:

Lord I thank you for sharing your heart of compassion with the examples in the Word. Give me that heart of compassion so I can see through your eyes and respond even as you did when there was a need before You. Amen.

ADDITIONAL READING: Exodus 2:6; Deuteronomy 30:3; 1 Samuel 23:14–29; 1 Kings 8:50; Psalm 78:38; Psalm 86:15; Psalm 111:4; Psalm 112:4; Psalm 145:8; Jeremiah 12:15; Lamentations 3:32; Micah 7:19; Romans 9:15; Hebrews 5:2; 10:34; 1 Peter 3:8; 1 John 3:17; Jude 1:22.

HIS WISDOM

There is a difference between knowledge and wisdom. For instance, my ability to fix a broken vehicle is almost zero. I may have some limited knowledge but without understanding and training, any bit of knowledge is basically useless. So wisdom is extremely important, especially in the days of great turmoil on the earth.

Let me ask this question: which well are you drawing from—the wisdom of man or the wisdom of God? It was God's idea to create us in the first place, so does it not make sense to check out His wisdom before someone else's? People pride themselves in higher learning, they have their own ideologies, their own belief systems, their own philosophies. What really troubles me is that if you line up their belief system against God's Word, and one piece of their belief system does not line up with the Word, that system has missed the mark. It is worth your effort to seek out the Word that expresses God's wisdom, His desire, His purpose, His plan, and His desire to create mankind in the first place.

If you are a believer or even considering the message of the gospel through Jesus the Son of God, you need to understand that God is all wisdom. Man's religious attempts to understand God have been foolish. The wisdom from above, the heavenly realm, cannot be compared to man's wisdom. For it says in Scripture that the wisdom of this world is foolishness with God (1 Corinthians 3:19).

God's wisdom ministers to the spirit, while knowledge appeals to the mind, emotions and will.

Perhaps you have heard the story in the book of Genesis of a garden called Eden. In it grew two specific trees among many other trees, shrubs and flowers: one was called "the knowledge of good and evil" while the other tree was called "the tree of life." If you ate from the knowledge of good and evil tree, you would die. One day, a crafty, sly snake came slithering near where the woman Eve was hanging out. 'Eve, hey look at that beautiful tree over there. The fruit is loaded with delicious fruit. You won't die if you just try one piece. Anyhow, did God really say you can't try some?'

She pondered and looked at the tree again and noticed how absolutely ready for the picking this fruit appeared.

Then the cunning and seducing snake spoke again, 'Come on, Eve, this tree produces such great fruit. I promise you it will make you wise;

you will be like God. You are actually going to be able to see clearly the difference between good and evil. Who doesn't like that idea?'

Eve's emotions must have been exploding inside of her. She had a choice to make. Should I or shouldn't I? Life or death? She decided to try some and then tell her husband later. So she did. After Adam ate some too, the Bible says that suddenly, their eyes were opened.

They were now operating on the deception of "man's wisdom" versus "God's wisdom."

Adam and Eve realized they were naked and they hid from God. When God confronted them, they blamed one another and the serpent.

God sent both Adam and Eve out of this perfect garden and placed an angel at the east gate of Eden, as well as a flaming sword which turned every way to guard the way to the tree of life.

Communication between people and God was broken. God knew all along He would have to make a way of redemption for His creation. It was not in God's plan to make robots, but people with a will to choose God the creator, or not.

We don't always choose God's wisdom. 1 Corinthians 1:18–25 says:

For the message of the cross is foolishness to those who are perishing, but to us who are being saved it is the power of God. For it is written: "I will destroy the wisdom of the wise, and bring to nothing the understanding of the prudent." Where is the wise? Where is the scribe? Where is the disputer of this age? Has not God made foolish the wisdom of this world? For since, in the wisdom of God, the world through wisdom did not know God, it pleased God through the foolishness of the message preached to save those who believe. For Jews request a sign, and Greeks seek after wisdom; but we preach Christ crucified, to the Jews a stumbling block and to the Greeks foolishness, but to those who are called, both Jews and Greeks, Christ the power of God and the wisdom of God. Because the foolishness of God is wiser than men, and the weakness of God is stronger than men.

In the Bible, Solomon is spoken of as the wisest man who ever lived, because He asked for God's wisdom. The results of that choice were astounding. He built the temple with God's wisdom.

One day, Solomon had a situation when two women came to him. They had each had a baby but one of the babies had died. The woman whose baby had died switched the live baby and put her dead baby with the other sleeping mother. They came to King Solomon to determine who was the real mother. God gave Solomon wisdom as to what he should do to find the truth: Solomon said he would take his sword and cut the baby in half. The true mother of the living child begged him not use the sword but to give the baby to the other woman. Solomon then knew who the true mother was: the one who was willing to give up her child so the child could live. With that, the right mother got her child back. All of Israel heard of this judgment by King Solomon and they feared the king, for they saw that the wisdom of God was in him to administer justice.[1]

In Luke 2:40 Jesus is described as a child that *"grew and became strong in spirit, filled with wisdom; and the grace of God was upon Him."* In the temple the teachers were astonished at the wisdom that flowed out of Jesus. And then in verse fifty-two: *"And Jesus increased in wisdom and stature, and in favor with God and men."*

The Apostle Paul spoke in Romans 11:33–36:

Oh, the depth of the riches both of the wisdom and knowledge of God! How unsearchable are His judgments and His ways past finding out! "For who has known the mind of the Lord? Or who has become His counselor?" "Or who has first given to Him and it shall be repaid to him?" For of Him, and through Him, and to Him are all things, to whom be glory forever. Amen.

The encouragement to me is that in James 1:5–8:

If any of you lacks wisdom, let him ask of God, who gives to all liberally and without reproach, and it will be given to him. But let him ask in faith, with no doubting, for he who doubts is like a wave of the sea driven and tossed by the wind. For let not that man suppose that he will receive anything from the Lord; he is a double-minded man, unstable in all his ways.

---

1   1 Kings 3: 16-28

The access to draw on God's wisdom is available to all who believe in Him. Just ask. Seek Him with all your heart. For out of the abundance of the heart, the mouth speaks.

ADDITIONAL READING: Job 28:1–28 (note verses 27–28); Job 38–41; Psalm 90:12; Psalm 104:24–35; Psalm 136:5–26; Proverbs 1:1–7, Exodus 31:1–11; Exodus 35–36.

HIS HOLINESS

As I began to prepare my heart to start writing this section of the book, I had an overwhelming sense to bow low before God for God is holy! It is very hard for me to describe what I was sensing. As the manifest presence of God began to invade the very room I sat in, I began to weep and cry aloud, "Holy, holy, holy!" There was nothing else I was able to say or do. Then I saw a picture of the heavenly realm where Jesus is sitting on the throne, and out of Him are shots of light like bright arrows, and angels singing and shouting loudly, "Holy, holy, holy! He is Pure, He is power, He is radiant, He is glorious, He is life, He is love, He reigns, He is holy."

Then I heard Him say, "Sit with Me. Come. There is a place for you. This is your inheritance. I paid the price."

As I walked toward Him, my knees were weak, but the closer I came to Him, the more strength came into me. Then He said, "I am your strength, I am your refuge, I am your strong tower.

There is a Scripture that confirms all that I experienced:

For if the firstfruit is holy, the lump is also holy; and if the root is holy, so are the branches. And if some of the branches were broken off, and you, being a wild olive tree, were grafted in among them, and with them became a partaker of the root and fatness of the olive tree, do not boast against the branches. But if you do boast, remember that you do not support the root, but the root supports you.

—Romans 11:16–18

CHAPTER TEN
The Temple God is Building

FOR YEARS, I CONDEMNED MY PHYSICAL BODY. WHY? BECAUSE THE WORLD out there says our goal should be to have a lean, thin body. My condemnation of my body allowed a foothold where I experienced frustration and confusion, not peace. When I thought about my body, I would never feel worthy before God, because I would feel like a failure. See how tricky the enemy is? But we know that he is a liar and a deceiver. No truth can come out of his mouth. Satan is defeated, period! Therefore, there is now no condemnation for those who are in Christ. I realized I had been walking in the flesh regarding this area of who I really am. I am holy, because God says I am holy. Hallelujah! I don't need to struggle or strain, or feel defeat—instead I am an overcomer (Revelations 3:12–13) through Christ who has strengthened me!

I want to look at the way God sees us instead. In 1 Corinthians 3:16–17, he says:

Do you not know that you are the temple of God and that the Spirit of God dwells in you? If anyone defiles the temple of God, God will destroy him. For the temple of God is holy, which temple you are.

The temple that He is building is holy, for He is holy. We are that temple. It is a spiritual temple He's building, not like a physical temple Solomon built, or the Tabernacle Moses built. They were the type and shadow of the true holy temple, which is you and I who believe in the finished work of Jesus Christ. So now the emphasis is not our physical body but the true temple which is spiritual. I believe we should be good stewards of our physical body, but far greater is this holy Body, who we are.

The temple God is building is pure, holy, and without any blemish. That's who God is. This new nature God is building is all that too. This process is happening from glory to glory, and faith to faith. There are no words to describe the honour He has placed upon us. He loves us so much. His love is eternal. So I give Him what is due: all honour and glory and power and dominion.

God is not only building a temple but also a city, what the Bible calls the New Jerusalem. To read about this we turn to Revelations 21 and the vision of this holy city:

> *Then I, John, saw the holy city, New Jerusalem, coming down out of heaven from God, prepared as a bride adorned for her husband. And I heard a loud voice from heaven saying, "Behold, the tabernacle of God is with men, and He will dwell with them, and they shall be His people. God Himself will be with them and be their God.*
>
> —Revelations 21:2,3

In Revelation 21:9, an angel said to John, "*Come, I will show you the bride, the Lamb's wife.*" What the angel shows John is the holy New Jerusalem; John saw this city descending out of heaven from God, having the glory of God, and described it as being a bride adorned for her husband. This image shows us that it's really about exalting the Father through Jesus the Groom, and us as His Bride. The husband and wife when getting married become one. Likewise, Jesus the groom and us the Bride are one.

And what is this city/bride like?

- The city/bride has the glory of God: it expresses His divine nature in and through us.

- Her light was like a most precious stone, like a polished jasper stone, clear as crystal and with no blemish.

- The city/bride had a great and high wall with twelve gates, and names written on them, which are the names of the twelve tribes of the children of Israel.

- The wall of the city has twelve foundations and on the foundation of each were written the twelve apostles of the Lamb (this city is established on the apostles and the prophets, Jesus Christ being the chief cornerstone. See Ephesians 2:19–22).

- The city, when measured by the angel who used a golden reed, was equal in measurement, laid out as a square. This measure shows us that God's holy city is built with equality, where all are equally valued, equally honoured.

- The city was pure gold, like clear glass. When we see gold in the Bible, it often represents God's divine nature, His glory (Job 23:10; Song of Solomon 5:1–16, Exodus 39:8–30; Exodus 40:5,26; Leviticus 8:9; Leviticus 24:6; Numbers 4:11; 1 Kings 6; 1 Kings 7: 48–51; Haggai 2: 6–9; Malachi 3:1–3; Matthew 2:11; Hebrews 9; Revelation 1; Revelation 3:18; Revelation 4:4; Revelation 5: 1–14; Revelation 14:14–16).

- The foundations of the wall of the city are adorned with all kinds of precious stones. These stones represent Jesus' priestly glory, and perfection on behalf of His people. I believe the value of each stone and foundation typifies the special value and significance of the believer to God who is building His abode in us.

- The city has twelve gates, each made of a pearl. Jesus referred to someone who sold all he had for a pearl of great price (Matthew 13:45–46). We can also think of how a pearl is formed over time, just as we grow over time in our faith until Christ is formed in us (Galatians 4:19; Isaiah 29:15–16; Isaiah 43:1–21; Isaiah 54:16–17; Romans 9:20–21).

- The city has one street, and it is made of pure gold that is like transparent glass. What demonstrates this on earth now is a lifestyle which comes from this one street which is like pure gold, like transparent glass, from God who dwells in us. This is the divine nature, the DNA that was planted into our spirit, when we were born again.

This city, the Bride adorned for her Husband, reveals the glory of God, drawing people to God. For the harvest is ripe and ready to be brought in. It will be and will require a Bride who is adorned for her Husband. This is the body that God delights in.

CHAPTER ELEVEN
God's Vision

SEEING GOD'S PERSPECTIVE, HIS HEART, HIS PURPOSE, HIS PLAN IS WHAT YOU begin to embrace when the Holy Spirit plants His seed into your spirit. In fact, God's vision is His redemption story about you and about me. When I repent, believe, and am baptized in the Name of Jesus, I have in fact chosen to embrace His vision.

God had a vision long before He even created mankind or the earth, planets, galaxies, sun, moon and stars. He is a God of vision in the eternal realm. You and I live temporarily in space and time, but have a spirit that is eternal. Why then did God bother making us with a physical body? Because He said in Genesis, "*Let us make man in our image*" (Genesis 1:26). It was for His pleasure. In order to produce mankind, He used physical processes to create us physically, but also with a soul and spirit.

Religious teaching has for a long time now told us that we have a dual nature, but this is not true. The old nature was nailed to the cross and that we are now a new creation (if we continue to try to get better and more holy, we will keep trying until we are literally worn out).

This new creation would have never been necessary unless Adam and Eve, who had a free will to choose just as we do, chose to disobey God and began to operate out of this sin nature. Redemption through Jesus was necessary to bring us back to right fellowship with God who created us in the first place. God's vision provided a way when we became born again through the Spirit. We also have His vision imparted into us through that seed.

Scripture says, *"My people are destroyed for lack of knowledge"* (Hosea 4:6) but God is increasing His revelations because that is the key and heart of God: to restore Jews and Gentiles all over the earth. We are closer than ever to the end of the end–times.

Your personal vision, plans and ideas are part of your old nature mentality. When you become a new creature in Christ, however, *"… old things have passed away; behold, all things have become new"* (2 Corinthians 5:17). That's where the doctrine of repentance has been lacking in most people's lives. Repentance means making an about–face and looking to Jesus, the author and finisher of your faith. You now have the DNA of Jesus; you can operate with the mind of Christ, thinking like Him and speaking like Him. But until you see the heart of God, His vision, you will stumble along.

The Bible says we are to renew our mind daily with the Word of God (Romans 12:2). The Bible says:

> *I have been crucified with Christ; it is no longer I who live, but Christ lives in me; and the life which I now live in the flesh I live by faith in the Son of God…*
>
> —Galatians 2:20

When you find this out, you know that the struggle of the flesh will fade. The Word is food that builds you up in your most holy faith.

God is a visionary, and always has been. Read the following Scriptures to see God's vision through visionary leaders:

> *Then the Angel of the LORD called to Abraham a second time out of heaven, and said: "By Myself I have sworn, says the LORD, because you have done this thing, and have not withheld your son, your only son—blessing I will bless you, and multiplying I will multiply your descendants as the stars of the heaven and as the sand which is on the seashore; and your descendants shall possess the gate of their enemies. In your seed all the nations of the earth shall be blessed, because you have obeyed My voice."*
>
> —Genesis 22:15–18

And if you are Christ's, then you are Abraham's seed, and heirs accord-
ing to the promise.

—Galatians 3:29

God instructed Moses to build the Tabernacle in Exodus 25–40, as a type and shadow of the tabernacle we are in Jesus Christ:

Who serve the copy and shadow of the heavenly things, as Moses was
divinely instructed when he was about to make the tabernacle. For He
said, "See that you make all things according to the pattern shown you
on the mountain."

—Hebrews 8:5

See also Hebrews 9: 6–15, 23–26; Hebrews 10:1–39; 1 Corinthians 10:1–11; Colossians 2: 16–17.

Solomon was a visionary. When he took over the kingship from David, he prayed for wisdom, God's wisdom. The result was the building of Solomon's temple, a type and shadow of the permanent corporate temple we are being built into when we receive this new creation spirit, which is the DNA of God.

The old covenant was a type and shadow of the vision to come; but God knew He would become the last will and testament, eternally. You and I are now partakers of that new covenant. What a visionary our God is!

When you and I embrace the end–time harvest, we come from the position of the heart of the Father God's heart. His love was exhibited by sending His Son Jesus. He paid the penalty we should have paid. All this was done out of love and vision: God's visionary heart. It took such kind of love to redeem us from death to life. Jesus' righteousness was placed upon us to bring us back in right standing with God. God's vision and God's love propels us forward into the harvest of souls because we have the greatest news any person can hear and experience: the gospel of the Lord Jesus Christ.

Part of the new covenant has to do with priesthood. God says of us that we have been made kings and priests:

But you are a chosen generation, a royal priesthood, a holy nation, His own special people, that you may proclaim the praises of Him who called you out of darkness into His marvelous light; who once were not a people but are now the people of God, who had not obtained mercy but now have obtained mercy.

—1 Peter 2:9–10

To Him who loved us and washed us from our sins in His own blood, and has made us kings and priests to His God and Father, to Him be glory and dominion forever and ever. Amen.

—Revelation 1:5–6

And they sang a new song, saying: You are worthy to take the scroll, and to open its seals; For You were slain and have redeemed us to God by Your blood out of every tribe and tongue and people and nation, and have made us kings and priests to our God; and we shall reign on the earth.

—Revelation 5:9–10

The seed that was planted in our spirit when we became born again caused us to be partakers of the kingship and royalty that is in Jesus Christ. Who would have dreamed such honour was placed upon us? This is the reality of being seated with Jesus on His throne. Now, heaven has come down to earth because we have the reality and substance of that truth in our spirit and have been made alive with His resurrection life to fulfill the vision and heart of God.

So, what does that kingly DNA look like as it's being worked out in our everyday lives? It is the revelation of knowing Jesus, the Word, when He declares: *"To him who overcomes I will grant to sit with Me on My throne, as I also overcame and sat down with My Father on His throne"* (Revelation 3:21).

The Laodicean church to whom Jesus was speaking in that Scripture were lukewarm believers. The outward actions of their faith were minimal. God is saying that if you seek Him first, before anything else, and make Him Lord of your life, He will grant you to sit with Him on His throne. The place is already there for you, but you just don't realize it. People are perishing for lack of knowledge and understanding of the living Word. So

He calls us to overcome, not by working our way up the ladder, but by acknowledging and opening ourselves up to The Living Word. As the Holy Spirit brings revelation and God's grace, He changes you. For He that has begun a good work in you will perform it unto the day of Jesus Christ. You shall know the truth, and the truth will set you free! (John 8:32) Embracing the Lord in these days will be vitally important as you grow in grace and in the knowledge of the Lord and Saviour Jesus Christ (Matthew 6:33; Philippians 1:6; Ephesians 2:8–9; John 8:32; 2 Peter 3:18).

When you begin to operate in the revelation knowledge and understanding, you operate with Jesus' authority, and a priestly servant heart. Your heart will operate in mercy, compassion, long–suffering, and more. You represent a kingdom, not of this world, but a kingdom from the heavenly realm with all authority that is coming down to the earthly realm through us. We represent Jesus who is priest and king after the order of Melchizedek (Hebrews 7: 13–17).

Jesus is the substance of this everlasting new covenant order. There is no sin in Him. This order of who we represent comes with an undivided heart for Jesus the Head, who is the way, the truth, and the life. This order does not express self–interest; it does not sit down and live in fear till Jesus comes, nor seeks a life of ease; it is not motivated by worldly power and money for self–motivation, but is always pressing into the Lord with His vision to be demonstrated through the Body. This Body is a remnant who is willing to surrender all, to doing the Father's will, always desiring to bring unity and oneness in love between the brethren. The Body does not demand biased opinions or have any prejudices which both trigger and stir up dissension in the Body.

Coming away into the inner chamber, that secret place (Psalm 91:1–16) will allow for Father God's heart and will to be fully matured in you. There is an intimacy we enter into where we know Christ is being formed into the fullness of Himself and something He has always intended for His creation. It is a place of ruling and reigning with Christ on the earth (Revelation 5:9–10).

Whatever spiritual level you are at, just know God's heart is for us all to keep moving forward from faith to faith, from glory to glory.

Wherever you are in your walk, sufficient grace is in you to always move forward. Just embrace Jesus with every part of your being.

Remember to ask yourself, "Where am I seated?" And know that you are seated in heavenly places with Jesus on His throne. That is part of the finished work He has provided.

Remind yourself in the following Scriptures how much God values you as His creation. Before the foundation of this world, He had a plan for you and I, to bring Him pleasure. We are the extension of His will and plan and vision.

Having predestined us to adoption as sons by Jesus Christ to Himself, according to the good pleasure of His will to the praise of the glory of His grace, by which He made us accepted in the Beloved.

—Ephesians 1:5–6

Having made known to us the mystery of His will, according to His good pleasure which He purposed in Himself.

—Ephesians 1:9

For it is God who works in you both to will and to do for His good pleasure.

—Philippians 2:13

Therefore we also pray always for you that our God would count you worthy of this calling, and fulfill all the good pleasure of His goodness and the work of faith with power.

—2 Thessalonians 1:11

For we are His workmanship, created in Christ Jesus for good works, which God prepared beforehand that we should walk in them.

—Ephesians 2:10

CHAPTER TWELVE
Truth

THERE ARE MANY VOICES CALLING OUT TO US—PERHAPS THOSE OF OUR parents, the computer, television, teachers or professors. Conflict rages in our minds while our moral compass is eroding. Why can I say that? Look at the fruit of people's lives. What are we demonstrating? I see a lot of "Let's eat drink and be merry, for tomorrow we die." People in general do not think about the future generation of kids growing up because the mindset is self–centredness and entitlement. The home for many kids is not a safe or soft place to fall. I see people demonstrating a desperation that shows they really do not know where to turn. Even the light of Jesus among believers has grown dimmer and dimmer to the point where many people will not even darken the door of a church building. They are saying, "They are no different than me. The God they are talking about, makes no difference in their lives. Give me something I can embrace and I might think about it."

Distrust and betrayal in our fellow man is proven every day, whether that is our family members, politicians, world leaders, business associates, etc. That isn't working. There is confusion, and people are unsettled, not knowing who or what to believe. So, who or what can I align myself with that even makes any sense at all, when it comes to truth? My desire is to be able to express truth not founded on my opinions, but on Someone who is called Truth. There must be something or someone we can align ourselves to that resonates with our spirit.

Every man, woman, teen and child is designed to search for something that is satisfying and fulfilling. People are trying to do this by running toward sex, drugs, alcohol, gangs, divorce, remarriage. But to no avail: that deep inner itch is not being fulfilled. Many don't realize this confusion and emptiness is spiritual.

I want to introduce you to a Person, not a religion, and His name is Jesus, He is truth. You see the religious crowd actually killed Him. But that did not work, because after three days, Jesus arose from the dead, and later went back to the Father. No other religion with their god or gods can declare that, because they were human beings and they are not God. So to say there is more than one way to heaven is a falsehood. Living good moral lives, or by following inner self truth, or any other excuse—none of these work. When one of Jesus' followers asked the way to heaven, Jesus said:

I am the way, the truth and the life. No one comes to the Father except through Me. If you had known Me, you would have known My Father also; and from now on, you know Him and have seen Him.

—John 14:6–7

Following Jesus is the only true way. God values the truth. He says:

"God is Spirit, and those who worship Him must worship in spirit and truth."

—John 4:24

However, when He, the Spirit of Truth, has come, He will guide you into all truth; for He will not speak on His own authority, but whatever He hears, He will speak; and He will tell you things to come. He will glorify Me, for He will take of what is Mine and declare it to you. All things that the Father has are Mine. Therefore I said that He will take of Mine and declare it to you.

—John 16:13–15

For you were once darkness, but now you are light in the Lord. Walk as children of light (for the fruit of the Spirit is in all goodness, righteousness, and truth), finding out what is acceptable to the Lord.

—Ephesians 5:8–10

But we are bound to give thanks to God always for you, brethren beloved by the Lord, because God from the beginning chose you for salvation through sanctification by the Spirit and belief in the truth, to which He called you by our gospel, for the obtaining of the glory of our Lord Jesus Christ. Therefore, brethren, stand fast and hold the traditions which you were taught, whether by word or our epistle.

—2 Thessalonians 2:13–15

This last passage is an interesting one. The writer, Paul, before he came into the truth of Jesus, had been called Saul, and was a highly learned religious Pharisee who was out to kill many Christians. Then he had an experience being blinded by light one day on the road to Damascus. The light was so bright, it knocked him to the ground and he became blind for a few days. During that time on the ground, God spoke to him through that light. Saul's spiritual eyes were opened and called Jesus Lord. Now you know something very profound and real happened to him that day.

By the time Paul was exhorting and encouraging the Thessalonian church years later, Paul had had a life–changing experience, and had grown in much grace, knowledge and wisdom in the person of the Lord Jesus Christ. He knew Jesus was the Truth, and he preached the true gospel of Jesus Christ where he had once persecuted the Christians

David cried out to the Lord:

Show me Your ways, O Lord; Teach me Your paths. Lead me in Your truth and teach me, for you are the God of my salvation; On You I wait all the day.

—Psalm 25:4–5

Other Psalms show us God is truth: *"All the paths of the Lord are mercy and truth, to such as keep His covenant and His testimonies"* (Psalm 25:10); *"The entirety of Your Word is truth, and every one of Your righteous judgments endures forever"*(Psalm 119:160).

In Proverbs 3:1–35, Solomon spoke words of wisdom, and in verse three, he said, *"Let not mercy and truth forsake you...."* Our lives will demonstrate truth, not just with words but with actions. This is why we engage in intercessory prayer for the peoples of the world who have yet to come to the living Truth: they must be given the opportunity to hear the good news of the gospel. He is *"...not willing that any should perish, but that all should come to repentance"* (2 Peter 3:9).

We must ask Holy Spirit to open their eyes to the Truth. So when the time comes for us to speak the Truth to them, the ground has been prepared to receive the Seed of Truth.

CHAPTER THIRTEEN

Giving

WHEN YOU READ THE TITLE OF THIS CHAPTER, YOU PROBABLY THOUGHT WE
would be talking about money, and you are partly right.

GIVING

For years I heard, "It's money that makes the world go around." After
all, money brings security for my family, it keeps businesses afloat, and
can make me rich. The problem is that one day you will die, and you
can't take it with you. So hoarding money and keeping it for yourself
truly is not the best decision in the big scheme of things.

If you don't give some of it away now, someone is going to get
your money when you're gone, whether it is your family, friends, or
the government.

One weekend, we had a team of prophetic ministry come into the
church and I was one of quite a few who were ministered to. One of
the prophets said, "Your giving is a sweet–smelling savour unto Me..."

Giving can be either for the right motivation or a wrong motivation. I was at a conference with the church family that I am a part of,
and prophetic word of encouragement came forward as I was called up.
The minister said to me, "Sister, I see an advertising sign and it says, 'You
Are Richer Than You Think!' That's the Word of the Lord over you."
I thought about it for some time, and one day that word came to my
memory and realized that wealth is not necessarily just about money,
although it can be. Being rich can be so much more than money; we can

be rich in compassion for the lost, we can be rich in our prayer life, rich in the Word of God, rich in counsel, rich in wisdom, rich in grace. I am sure you get the point. When you are hooked in with the Lord and He's hooked in with you, you are truly richer than you think. So if I have shaken your mindset on being rich, that's a good thing. Challenging one's thinking can positively move you forward in your relationship with the Lord. Some verses to keep in mind:

A good man leaves an inheritance to his children's children, but the wealth of the sinner is stored up for the righteous.

—Proverbs 13:22

As for every man to whom God has given riches and wealth, and given him power to eat of it, to receive his heritage and rejoice in his labor— this is the gift of God.

—Ecclesiastes 5:19

Then you shall see and become radiant, and your heart shall swell with joy; because the abundance of the sea shall be turned to you, the wealth of the Gentiles shall come to you.

—Isaiah 60:5

"The silver is Mine, and the gold is Mine," says the Lord of hosts. "The glory of this latter temple shall be greater than the former," says the Lord of hosts. "And in this place I will give peace," says the Lord of hosts.

—Haggai 2:8–9

CHARITY

If you have been around the church, I am sure you will be familiar with 1 Corinthians 13. We mostly hear that chapter read at weddings because it is a chapter about love. The word for love is also translated as charity and really this word, charity, fits into every aspect of one's life. When you are at your place of employment, in your family setting, when your relatives come to your home for the weekend, when you get on the transit bus, or are driving your car down the street, you are in a place to be charitable. Charity is part of God's nature.

Webster's Dictionary explains charity this way: "generous to the needy, benevolent, lenient in judging others, tolerant, kindly" while Strong's Concordance says it means to love in a social or moral sense. Charity is an action word.

My husband and I bought some undeveloped property where neighbours lived on either side of us. The family north of the property had been there for years. Their religious background involved not eating any meat whatsoever. They were actually missionaries originally from the USA. They were lovely people, but I knew they were bound and determined to convert us to their religious belief system. One day we invited them all over for a visit and lunch. I made a very deliberate decision not to serve meat at the luncheon. At one point, the lady said that I was not really born again unless I kept the Sabbath. This meant everything would have to stop on our working ranch from sundown Friday to sundown Saturday. I did not want to debate the subject, so I found a way of changing the subject. They told us they had lost a son through a farm accident. It was very devastating for the whole family and they indicated they would like another child, but were fearful something would happen again. Father God spoke to me and told me to ask them if it was okay to pray for them regarding their fear, and that if they would agree with me to pray for another child.

To my pleasant surprise, they said yes. I rebuked the spirit of fear in Jesus' name and commanded that spirit to stop harassing the whole family.

"Would you like a son?" I asked the lady. "Yes." she responded. She began to cry as I prayed, and she believed with me, and, praise God, in one month she was pregnant and in nine months she had a baby boy.

This is an example of being lenient in judging others and instead being charitable and loving them where they are at. God teaches us how to do this:

I know and am convinced by the Lord Jesus that there is nothing unclean of itself; but to him who considers anything to be unclean, to him it is unclean. Yet if your brother is grieved because of your food, you are no longer walking in love. Do not destroy with your food the one for whom Christ died. Therefore do not let your good be spoken of as evil; for the kingdom of God is not eating and drinking, but righteousness and peace and joy in the Holy Spirit.

—Romans 14:14–17

God is our source for everything. If money becomes an idol, the Lord takes second place. It might be time to make the necessary mindset adjustments. Friend, there is nothing wrong with money. But you are not just rich because you have money but your abundance, richness, charity, and giving hinges upon God's love and grace for you. We generously respond out of the richness of God's love. Don't put God in a box regarding being rich.

Finally, the greatest expression of giving, is seen in Father God sending His Son Jesus to redeem us to Himself. This giving is the highest expression possible, for there never was nor shall be anyone who will ever replace Jesus. It was finished, it is finished and shall be finished for all eternity! There is no blood that was shed that was perfect like His. He is the Lamb who took upon Himself the sin of the world. It was the perfect sacrifice, the Lamb. This is a free gift to all mankind, but it's not cheap.

Read these verses that show us the Father's gift to us:

But as many as received Him, to them He gave the right to become children of God, to those who believe in His name: who were born, not of blood, nor of the will of the flesh, nor of the will of man, but of God. And the Word became flesh and dwelt among us, and we beheld His glory, the glory as of the only begotten of the Father, full of grace and truth.

—John 1:12–14

For God so loved the world that He gave His only begotten Son, that whoever believes in Him should not perish but have everlasting life. For God did not send His Son into the world to condemn the world, but that the world through Him might be saved.

—John 3:16–17

For I have not spoken on My own authority; but the Father who sent Me gave Me a command, what I should say and what I should speak. And I know that His command is everlasting life. Therefore, whatever I speak, just as the Father has told me, so I speak.

—John 12:49–50

And the glory which You gave Me, I have given them, that they may be one just as We are one: I in them and You in Me; that they may be made perfect in one, and that the world may know that You have sent Me, and have loved them as You have loved Me.

—John 17:22–23

I pray you can see clearly now that the great giving of His Son Jesus Christ was a plan no man could have conceived. For when we receive of this abundance, *"the glory which You gave Me I have given them"* (John 17:22).

CHAPTER FOURTEEN

The Principle of the Tithe

IT'S NOT ABOUT MONEY. DO I HAVE YOUR ATTENTION? I'M SURE I DO.

I have thought about and been told over many years about the idea of the tithe, and possibly you have too. My hope and desire is that you will consider the Scriptural foundation of the tithe and be willing to let go of some mindsets that have not given you any peace.

Here are some comments that plagued my thinking. Possibly you have thought many of the same thoughts:

- I'm a believer. I have to tithe, because if I don't, I won't be blessed.
- If you want to be a voting member and remain in our church, one of the prerequisites is that you must tithe.
- Malachi 3:8-12 says you must tithe.
- No, we are in the New Covenant; tithing isn't mentioned there.
- No, tithe was under the law, but now we are under grace.
- You give according to 2 Corinthians 9:7, "*Let each man give as he purposes in his heart, not grudgingly or of necessity; for God loves a cheerful giver.*"

You might be thinking it's all very confusing.

My personal mindset has swung from tithing under the law to giving as I have purposed in my heart, not grudgingly, or of necessity, for God loves a cheerful giver. I used to tithe out of guilt, to the extreme that

I determined to give whenever I felt like it. I was ridiculed for tithing and was told that all that the church wants is your money, that we couldn't afford to tithe.

I was in a dilemma, and maybe you are now as well. My hope and prayer is that you will receive clarity and revelation as you come with me on this journey and discover what God's Word really says about the tithe.

What if I told you that tithing has nothing to do with money?

Have you ever heard of Melchizedek? Let's look at a few Scriptures that show us why he is important in this scenario.

We read in Genesis that Abram had just won a battle against the enemy. He brought back all the goods, his brother Lot, as well as the women and the people. Someone appeared before him and did something very significant:

> *Then Melchizedek king of Salem brought out bread and wine; he was the priest of God Most High. And he blessed him and said, "Blessed be Abram of God Most High, Possessor of heaven and earth; And blessed be God Most High, who has delivered your enemies into your hand." And he gave a tithe of all.*
>
> —Genesis 14:18-20

In Psalm 110, David prophesies and announces the Messiah's reign. That whole chapter is very important to read and meditate on because David is proclaiming prophetically the truth of Jesus Christ, the Messiah found in the New Testament Scriptures. By faith, David was looking forward toward the Messiah, and we now look back to the confirmed King Jesus who is the Messiah: *"The Lord has sworn and will not relent, 'You are a priest forever according to the order of Melchizedek'"* (Psalm 110:4). Take note: that same Melchizedek that Abram gave the tithe to is the same Melchizedek David speaks of.

As we look further in Scripture let's go to the book of Hebrews in the New Testament:

> *So also Christ did not glorify Himself to become High Priest, but it was He who said to Him: "You are My Son, today I have begotten You."*

As He also says in another place: "You are a priest forever according to the order of Melchizedek; who, in the days of His flesh, when He offered up prayers and supplications, with vehement cries and tears to Him who was able to save Him from death, and was heard because of His godly fear, though he was a Son, yet learned he obedience by the things which he suffered. And having been perfected, he became the author of eternal salvation to all who obey Him, called by God as high priest, "according to the order of Melchizedek," of whom we have much to say, and hard to explain, since you have become dull of hearing.

—Hebrews 5:5-11

In Genesis 14:18, we read that Melchizedek brought bread and wine to Abram. Why bread and wine? In the Christian church service today, we will have what we call communion, the sharing of bread and wine, as described in 1 Corinthians 11:23-26. It's a time of honouring and remembering the shedding of Jesus' blood for our sins, and the stripes He took upon His back for all our sicknesses and diseases. We do this together as a group of believers to give thanks, praise and honour to our eternal, perfect, living sacrifice, Jesus Christ, our High Priest after the order of Melchizedek.

At that moment that Melchizedek gave Abram the bread and wine, Melchizedek was foretelling and pronouncing to Abram the gospel. Abram is our father in the faith. He participated with Melchizedek and a prayer of blessing was given over Abram. With such a revelation, we honour our high priest after the order of Melchizedek, as spoken of in Hebrews. Abram provided a tenth of all of the enemy spoils that day, in honour and gratitude for the help and grace of God (Genesis 14:20).

This is the first time the tithe was mentioned in the Bible, long before it was commanded in the Levitical priesthood under the Old Covenant some 430 years later.

In Abram, God shows us His awesome plan for the redemption for mankind. First God made a covenant with Abram in Genesis 15. God said to him, *"Do not be afraid, Abram. I am your shield, your exceedingly great reward"* (Genesis 15:1). Abram called Him "Adonai" which means Lord God. This title represents the idea of God's majesty that calls for honour, reverence, loyalty, and personal devotion. In the New Testament, Lord God is translated master or owner. In the next several verses, Abram tells the Lord God that he has no seed, no offspring. God responds by telling him to look at the sky, the heavens. "*Count the stars if you are able to number them…so shall your descendants be*" (Genesis 15:5) Abram "*believed in the Lord, and He accounted it to him for righteousness*" (Genesis 15:6). God would change his name to Abraham, meaning "*father of many nations*" (Genesis 17:5).

In the New Testament we read,

> *And the Scripture, foreseeing that God would justify the Gentiles by faith, preached the gospel to Abraham beforehand, saying, "In you all the nations shall be blessed." So then those who are of faith are blessed with believing Abraham…Now to Abraham and his Seed were the promises made. He does not say, "And to seeds," as of many, but as of one, "And to your Seed," who is Christ. And this I say, that the law, which was four hundred and thirty years later, cannot annul the covenant that was confirmed before by God in Christ, that it should make the promise of no effect. For if the inheritance is of the law, it is no longer of promise; but God gave it to Abraham by promise. What purpose then does the law serve? It was added because of transgressions, till the Seed should come to whom the promise was made; and it was appointed through angels by the hand of a mediator. Now a mediator does not mediate for one only, but God is one.*
>
> —Galatians 3:8-9, 16-20

Abraham's covenant is an eternal promised covenant for all who believe by faith. Abraham believed and was blessed not only with eternal life, but with great blessings. Remember that Abraham is our father in the faith. The Mosaic law could not annul the Abrahamic covenant; otherwise it is no promise with no guarantees.

Jesus is that better covenant after the order of Melchizedek. When Abram gave that tithe, he was giving it to honour God who through Jesus would provide a better covenant, an everlasting covenant. Abram's eyes were opened that day, and by faith, he entered in as he looked toward the better covenant. Melchizedek is that type and shadow of this better covenant, through Jesus Christ, our Redeemer, our High Priest after the order of Melchizedek.

My pastor made a very profound statement, "The tithe is the wedding ring of this new covenant." We are wed with Jesus. Just as the wedding ring is a token, the tithe is a covenant token of honour and reverence (read Ephesians 6:22-33 for further study). We, the Bride, and Jesus, the Groom, are united as one through this better covenant that happened through His death and resurrection.

With this understanding in mind, the tithe is given to the house of God (Genesis 28:10-22). According to verse seventeen, it's not only the house of God, but the gate to open heaven. In Jacob's dream, he sees a ladder that reached from earth to heaven. The angels were ascending and descending. Above the ladder, the Lord stood and said, "*I am the Lord God of Abraham your father, and the God of Isaac; the land on which you lie I will give to you and your descendants*" (Genesis 28:13).

The tithe of honour, the open heaven, the inheritance through Jesus Christ will provide a life of rest, revelation, destiny, purpose and blessing. This is a guarantee for the people who walk by faith, even as our father of faith Abraham did.

Let's conclude with Matthew 6:19-21:

Do not lay up for yourselves treasures on earth, where moth and rust destroy, and where thieves break in and steal; but lay up for yourselves treasures in heaven, where neither moth or rust destroys and where thieves do not break in and steal. For where your treasure is, there your heart will be also.

The tithe is about expressing honour and reverence to Jesus Christ, our High Priest after the order of Melchizedek. The tithe belongs to God; it's not ours. The tithe is not a seed, not an offering; it does not multiply. Giving is seed planted into lives or ministries to further and enhance the kingdom of God.

ADDITIONAL READING: Hebrews 7.

CHAPTER FIFTEEN

He is All Powerful, Majestic, and Full of Glory—And He Lives in Us!

The voice of the Lord is over the waters; The God of glory thunders; The Lord is over many waters. The voice of the Lord is powerful; The voice of the Lord is full of majesty.

—Psalm 29:3–4

DAVID THE PSALMIST SINGS PRAISES TO GOD WHO IS ALL HOLY AND ALL majestic. As David sings and worships God, I sense there must have been a tremendous weightiness of God's presence. That whole chapter declares the extravagance and abundance of who God is. David received revelation. Heaven opened for him. When David's spiritual eyes were opened up, he expressed the many attributes of who God is.

Hear what Jeremiah says about the awesomeness of our God:

He has made the earth by His power, He has established the world by His wisdom, and has stretched out the heavens at His discretion. When He utters His voice, there is a multitude of waters in the heavens: "And He causes the vapors to ascend from the ends of the earth. He makes lightning for the rain, He brings the wind out of His treasuries.

—Jeremiah 10:12–13

The Lord is all powerful. I think of Moses' encounter with Pharaoh in Egypt. In Exodus 6–10, God tells Moses to stand before Pharaoh. Moses declares several plagues, and it was so. God spoke through Moses and spoke to Pharaoh the following:

Now if I had stretched out My hand and struck you and your people with pestilence, then you would have been cut off from the earth. But, indeed for this purpose I have raised you up, that I may show My power in you, and that My name may be declared in all the earth.

—Exodus 9:15–16

Moses stretches out his hand toward heaven and declares plague after plague but Pharaoh's heart continued to be hard as he tried to manipulate Moses. As you can see "power" meant a lot to Pharaoh. This spirit still prevails today.

The exciting part of this story is that the children of Israel were protected and shown that God is a big, powerful and faithful God. Also, Pharaoh learned that God would indeed show mercy if he would shake his pride and let Israel go.

It is interesting that Paul declares in 1 Corinthians 4:20, *"For the kingdom of God is not in word but in power."*

David declares in a song, *"God is my strength and power, and He makes my way perfect"* (2 Samuel 22:33). David not only knew God's acts, but also His ways. His strength and power came from the heavenly realm, from God Himself.

After the Israelites left Egypt, God reminded the children of Israel how He had helped them get out of Egypt. By this time, they were living a very compromising lifestyle of idol worship and God showed them that they were training their children to follow that same path. God said:

But the Lord, who brought you up from the land of Egypt with great power and an outstretched arm, Him you shall fear, Him you shall worship, and to Him you shall offer sacrifice.

—2 Kings 17:36

Centuries later, David praised the Lord for His love and power:

Therefore David blessed the Lord before all the assembly; and David said: "Blessed are You, Lord God of Israel, our Father, forever and ever. Yours, O Lord, is the greatness, the power and the glory, the victory and the majesty; For all that is in heaven and in earth is Yours; Yours is the kingdom, O Lord, and You are exalted as head over all. Both riches and honor come from You, and You reign over all. In Your hand is power and might; In Your hand it is to make great and to give strength to all.

—1 Chronicles 29:10–12

I love David's heart, but more importantly, God loved his heart too. David acknowledged how great and powerful God is.

Let's take a look at Job. In Job 26, Job is talking about His frailty and God's majesty and power. Satan could not kill Job, but he sure did test him. Job declares this about God:

- You helped those without power
- You saved the arm that has no strength
- You counseled the one who has no wisdom
- You have declared sound advice to many
- You have uttered words and whose spirit came from you?
- The dead tremble and, those under the waters and those inhabiting them.
- Sheol is naked before Him
- Destruction has no covering.
- He stretches out the north over empty space
- He hangs the earth on nothing.
- He binds up the water in His thick clouds, yet the clouds are not broken under it.
- He covers the face of His throne and spreads His cloud over it.
- He drew a circular horizon on the face of the waters, at the boundary of light and darkness.
- The pillars of heaven tremble, and are astonished at His rebuke.
- He stirs up the sea with His power, and by His understanding, He breaks up the storm.
- By His Spirit He adorned the heavens.

- His hand pierced the fleeing serpent.
- The thunder of His power who can understand?

Job later says he will not allow his integrity to be soiled in any way. He knew his God. His faith and trust remained as long as he had breath.

As believers, we must keep things in perspective. God is all powerful, full of majesty and great glory. He has given His creation the position of sitting with Him on the right hand of the Father. We are His royal priesthood. As we always seek first the kingdom of God, His glory and majesty and power will come forth as we recognize it is no longer I who lives, but Christ in me. For the life that I now live, I live by faith of the Son of God. It is not about you or me, but all about Him. God has chosen to dwell in us. What an honour! Truly, this is the season for the manifestation of the sons of God. Why? To declare God's glory, His majesty, His power. My friends, embrace Him now, and allow His DNA to be released in Jesus' Name.

Just as a reminder to you again: what you have read so far regarding the planting of the seed is almost more than we can take in, but as you study this, allow the Holy Spirit to minister life and reveal truth as you meditate on the Word of God. As this eternal seed gets a hold of you and enlarges, the Holy Spirit will bring revelation and God's eternal plan with understanding. You, as an ambassador of this kingdom, will allow the enabling power of God, and His grace to be expressed to influence others in this lost and hopeless world. People are desperately crying for hope, and we who believe in Jesus Christ the Son of God have the answer. Let God's divine nature of kindness be the extraordinary in your sphere of influence.

ADDITIONAL READING: Psalm 21:13; Psalm 29:4; Psalm 49:15; Psalm 62:11; Psalm 63:2; Psalm 66:7; Isaiah 40:21–31; Jeremiah 32:16–22; Matthew 6: 9–13; Matthew 9:6–7; Matthew 9:8; Matthew 10:1; Matthew 22:29; Matthew 24:29–31; Mark 5:30; Luke 1:35; Luke 4:36–37; Luke 5:22–24; Luke 6:19; Luke 9:1–6; Luke 10:19–20; Luke 22:66–71; Luke 24:46–49; John 10:17; John 19:10–11; Acts 1:8; Acts 3:11–16; Acts

4:5–12; Acts 6:8; Acts 10:34–43; Romans 1:1–7; Romans 1:16; Romans 1:20; Romans 15:13,19; Revelation 1:6; Revelation 17:14.

CHAPTER SIXTEEN

The Extravagance of God's Grace

DO YOU WANT TO BE SET FREE FROM THE HEAVINESS OF BONDAGE, LAW, AND religion? When the revelation becomes clear and alive in you, you will never be the same again.

I have heard many preachers try to explain God's grace. As I look back now, their teaching really did not give me the freedom I experience now. My hope and prayer is that I am able to articulate clearly with God's power and anointing His awesome extravagance.

The Greek meaning of the word grace means the divine influence upon the heart and its reflection in life, gratitude, acceptableness, benefit, favour, gift, joy, liberality, pleasure, being thankworthy. The Hebrew meaning of grace means: kindness, favour, beauty, pleasantness, preciousness, being well–favoured.

If Jesus was in physical form as He was when He was walking this earth, I could introduce you like this. "It would be my honour to introduce you to Mr. Grace."

John 1:14,16 says:

And the Word became flesh and dwelt among us, and we beheld His glory, the glory as of the only begotten of the Father, full of grace and truth...And of His fullness we have all received, and grace for grace.

God has cloaked Himself in flesh, in you and me as believers. What an honour and privilege. Jesus the Word became flesh and dwelled among us; now Jesus the Word, dwells in us.

Jesus is full of grace and truth. That's who He is. He dwells in us through the Spirit. We are partakers of His grace and truth, receiving and being partakers of His DNA when we are born again. When the Holy Spirit begins to unwrap this truth to us, layer by layer, we will see how powerful and awesome His grace is in us.

There is a continual progression and revelation of grace as we walk this journey, which, by the way, never ends. This is the kind of grace that causes us to embrace Him as we seek to know His ways.

I want to make note of Luke's declaration when he said the grace of God was upon the child Jesus: "*And the Child grew and became strong in spirit, filled with wisdom; and the grace of God was upon Him*" (Luke 2:40). This grace of God embraced Jesus at a very young age. He operated in wisdom as the teachers in the temple found out. He asked them questions and He responded with great wisdom. The teachers surely recognized grace was upon Jesus, as seen in the Scriptures (John 1:47).

The early church was characterized by grace:

> *Now the multitude of those who believed were of one heart and one soul; neither did anyone say that any of the things he possessed was his own, but they had all things in common. And with great power the apostles gave witness to the resurrection of the Lord Jesus. And great grace was upon them all. Nor was there anyone among them who lacked; for all who were possessors of lands or houses sold them, and brought the proceeds of the things that were sold and laid them at the apostles' feet; and they distributed to each as anyone had need.*
>
> —Acts 4:32–35

This church operated with one heart and one soul. Liberality was the norm. Selfishness was not part of their vocabulary. When the pure motivation of the heart comes forward in action, then grace is manifest. The new church showed through their lives exceeding great grace: it spoke loudly, it spoke mightily; in fact great fear came upon all who saw and heard how grace was being demonstrated through obedient people. The atmosphere was electrifying with the power of God. Truly, the glory and majesty of God was seen loud and clear.

The first time I heard my pastor teach and preach on "honour" (meaning honouring one another, and equally honouring the Christ in each of us), the atmosphere of my heart changed. For this is the key to bringing what happened in Acts into this season we are in. To show great love and great honour through the enabling power of God will bring forward the action among every believer that will ultimately bring great glory to the Lord.

In the early church, as the continuing power of God in the church was manifest through signs and wonders, and many believers were added to the church. With all of this going on, the enemy was very angry and operated through the high priest and his helpers, the Sadducees, who ultimately imprisoned the apostles. But an angel of the Lord came and loosed them and freed them from prison. Soon they were back in the temple preaching the Word of the Lord.

The grace of God is so powerful it will bring God's influence to your heart, and will change your life.

CHAPTER SEVENTEEN

How To Mentor a New Disciple of Jesus Christ

JESUS TOLD HIS DISCIPLES:

> *I have been given all authority in heaven and earth. Therefore, go and make disciples of all the nations, baptizing them in the name of the Father and the Son and the Holy Spirit. Teach these new disciples to obey all the commands I have given you. And be sure of this: I am with you always, even to the end of the age.*
>
> —Matthew 28:18–20 (NLT)

When you meet a believer in Jesus Christ, and listen to them talk, you can discern their maturity very quickly by what comes out of the mouth. I know of believers who have been on their journey for fifty or sixty years who still talk at a baby level, and I wonder what has happened. The reality is that they have probably never been spiritually mentored. They pick up a few things from their church fellowship, but no one has really taken them under their wing.

Over the years I have observed a lack of discipleship training. Christians may lead someone to Christ and ask them to invite Jesus in their heart, but to actually take that one under their wing is hardly ever heard of. People basically think it is the pastor's job—we pay him or her—and now we can sit in the warm pews and gloat that we led someone to Jesus. It is sad, but it is true. It is my prayer that churches will have compassion upon every soul that comes and quickly move that baby believer to a safe and loving place where they can be given spiritual milk and encouraged to trust God for every moment of every day.

This means teaching by example, training them from the Word, praying with them, teaching them to obey the Word. It means not judging them when they fall down. Love them, pour into them until you see steadfastness and strong faith rising up from their spirit. Give them all the tools as a new believer. Pray that they will receive the infilling power of the Holy Spirit as the evidence of the power of God in them. Lay hands upon them to be filled with the Holy Spirit, with the evidence of speaking in tongues. Allow them to exercise their prayer language. Teach and show them how to pray for others by laying hands on someone for healing and deliverance for their soul or body.

As a mama, I know what it takes to raise a baby up to where they can begin to walk and feed themselves. As new parents bringing a baby home, you soon find this beautiful child wants to be fed every three hours. Do we do this for our new believer? Is it really any different? Where is our commitment for that special child of God? When you encourage a baby to walk, you generally help them up by holding them with both hands. Later at some point, you get them to come to you. They may fall, but you encourage them to get up, until they are able to walk, even though it may be wobbly in the beginning. So it is with a new believer.

Often we ourselves need the tools first before we can really disciple a new believer.

These are some of the questions a new believer may ask:

- What happens at birth?
- What does it mean to repent from dead works?
- How do I explain faith and trust in God?
- What is the point of the doctrines of water baptism and infilling of the Holy Spirit?
- Why is it necessary to be filled with the Holy Spirit?
- What is the resurrection of the dead and eternal judgment?
- How about prayer communion?
- How to hear God's voice?
- How about fellowshipping with people of like faith?

- How about going out and sharing Christ with others?
- How about forgiveness and loving your neighbour?
- How forgiven are you? Can I lose my salvation?
- How powerful is God's grace in me?

Let's address some of these questions:

1. WHAT IS REPENTANCE FROM DEAD WORKS?

According to the Scriptures, every true believer must repent from dead works. Hebrews 5:12–6:2 explains:

> *For though by this time you ought to be teachers, you need someone to teach you again the first principles of the oracles of God; and you have come to need milk and not solid food. For everyone who partakes only of milk is unskilled in the word of righteousness, for he is a babe. But solid food belongs to those who are of full age, that is, those who by reason of use have their senses exercised to discern both good and evil. Therefore, leaving the discussion of the elementary principles of Christ, let us go on to perfection, not laying again the foundation of repentance from dead works and of faith toward God, of the doctrine of baptisms, of laying on of hands, of resurrection of the dead, and of eternal judgment.*

Anyone who knows the structural elements of building a house will know that the foundation is essential to laying a solid foundation for the rest of the house to stand firm. So repentance from dead works and of faith toward God are the basics. For now, I am focusing on repentance from dead works.

Conversion is that change of mind (repentance) of the sinner in which he/she turns from sin to Jesus Christ. What you are doing is doing a turn–about face or turning toward Jesus Christ. It's like you were walking in death and now you are walking in life—the life of Jesus. The beginning of our salvation happens when a person is converted from the dominion of Satan unto the Lordship of Jesus Christ.

Repentance means the act of repenting or the state of being penitent, sorrow or regret for what has been done or left undone by oneself; especially, sorrow and contrition for sin; there is remorse. Remorse says a person feels godly sorrow for sin and is willing to forsake that old life. One little boy said it meant "being sorry enough to quit." Repentance is an attitude and a way of life, bringing about a complete or full change of mind.

There are actually three elements of repentance:

1. Intellectual: change of view—the mind
2. Emotional : change of feeling—the emotions
3. Volitional: change of purpose—the will

The Holy Spirit's responsibility is the one that leads us to repentance (godly sorrow); it is a gift. It also Scriptural to say that the goodness of God leads us to repentance (Romans 2:4). 2 Corinthians 7:10 teaches us, *"For godly sorrow produces repentance leading to salvation, not to be regretted; but the sorrow of the world produces death."*

Paul in Acts 20:17–21 exhorted the Ephesian elders that although he was going through trials and many tears because of the plotting of the Jew,; he kept back nothing that was helpful, but proclaimed to them and taught from house to house and publicly, testifying to the Jews and also to the Greeks repentance toward God and faith in our Lord Jesus Christ.

Paul again spoke to King Agrippa; he was not disobedient to the heavenly vision, but declared first to those in Damascus and in Jerusalem, and throughout all the region of Judea, and then to the Gentiles that they should repent, turn to God and do works befitting repentance. (Acts 26:19–20).

Paul taught his student Timothy:

And a servant of the Lord must not quarrel but be gentle to all, able to teach, patient, in humility correcting those who are in opposition, if God perhaps will grant them repentance so that they may know the truth, and that they may come to their senses and escape the snare of the devil, having been taken captive by him to do his will.

—2 Timothy 2:24–26

Here Paul was exhorting Timothy to teach and train his workers to be diligent to present yourself approved to God, a worker who does not need to be ashamed, rightly dividing the word of truth. Train them not to strive about words that will lead to no profit. Avoid profane babblings for it will only lead to more ungodliness. This message will spread like cancer.

Repentance is not a negative word, but rather a word that will lead us toward God. He is the one who paid the price for our salvation, through Jesus Christ's obedience. Faith then must accompany repentance. True repentance cannot truly be experienced without faith toward God. Faith is in the finished work of Christ; His death, burial, resurrection and ascension will bring about true repentance.

Repentance is the gift of God. It is God who takes the initiative in repentance. It does not originate with us. No man can or will repent of himself. It is the very grace of God, through the Holy Spirit who convicts people to bring us to a state of repentance. Our part is simply to respond to God's conviction. God commands mankind to repent. If He commands, He will also enable us to respond (Acts 11:18; Acts 5:30–31; 2 Timothy 2:25). True repentance will be seen by the fruit in one's life.

2. WHAT IS FAITH?

Faith is believing and seeing the invisible, and expecting it to manifest in the natural. God teaches us about faith when he says:

> *Now faith is, the substance of things hoped for, the evidence of things not seen. For by it the elders obtained a good testimony. By faith we understand that the worlds were framed by the word of God, so that the things which are seen were not made of things which are visible.*
> —Hebrews 11:1–2

We have physical eyes, but also spiritual eyes—those are your faith eyes. The spiritual eyes believe that God exists; your spiritual eyes see the invisible by faith. In fact, the spiritual is more real than the physical, for the spiritual has always existed, whereas God created the world with His spoken Word at a certain season of time. By faith, you speak to the mountain and it will be removed. God honours faith. This mountain may be your finances, a negative family situation, a business partner or worker tiff, or a government crisis in your country. The new covenant has provided a way to see this situation change for the good. By faith you believe that Jesus came and provided His redemption plan before the foundation of this world. He provides the hope and assurance of His faithfulness. That is why you can be fully confident that our God has a way to help you with every situation you may go through.

Faith and patience are like identical twins. With faith you can expect patience may be required. Having that snap–my–fingers attitude and demanding God to do it this very second may not always happen so don't become impatient. In order for faith to grow and mature, there may need to be an extended time period for patience. You never give up for you know in whom you believe, and are fully persuaded that He is faithful to do what He said He will do.

On a personal level, I exercised faith with someone regarding a situation when suddenly it happened in front of our eyes. That was pretty awesome. Another time, I prayed for thirty–two years for the answer, and kept believing before it came to pass. That was an example of patience. But it caused my faith to stay secure in God who, of course, is my source. God's timing and my timing were definitely different but I chose to look through the eyes of faith. God takes great pleasure and smiles when we trust Him, and Him alone.

Embrace these verses:

My brethren, count it all joy when you fall into various trials, knowing that the testing of your faith produces patience. But let patience have its perfect work, that you may be perfect and complete, lacking nothing. If any of you lacks wisdom, let him ask of God, who gives to all liberally and without reproach, and it will be given to him. But let him ask in faith, with no doubting, for he who doubts is like a wave of the sea driven and tossed by the wind. For let not that man suppose that he will receive anything from the Lord; he is a double–minded man, unstable in all his ways.

—James 1:2–8

Never lose heart when you are seeing with eyes of the invisible. As God's Word says:

Therefore we do not lose heart. Even though our outward man is perishing, yet the inward man is being renewed day by day. For our light affliction, which is but for a moment, is working for us a far more exceeding and eternal weight of glory, while we do not look at the things which are seen, but at the things which are not seen. For the things which are seen are temporary, but the things which are not seen are eternal.
—2 Corinthians 4:16–18

God is faithful!

ADDITIONAL READING: Colossians 1:15–18; Hebrews 11:6–7; Romans 3:3–4

So take time to build up yourselves in your most holy faith, specifically, the faith of the Son of God (Galatians 2:20). Spend regular time in the Word of God so you will not be moved by anything that may come into your path. For Jesus said in the last days, "*…will He really find faith in the earth?*" (Luke 18:8).

Do you believe when you get up in the morning that the sun will rise in the east and go down in the west? Do you have faith when you sit in the airplane and the plane lifts off that you will reach your destination? You say, "I trust the mechanics and that they did their job right." It does take faith, even if you don't think about it. Do you have faith when you put your feet on the floor that your legs and feet will hold the rest of the body vertical as you begin to walk? Let's be totally honest, we kind of take things for granted, but it does take a certain amount of faith even though we may not acknowledge it.

I have always been fascinated that when I put a seed in the ground, pour some water on it, and see the warm sun hit the soil, a week or so later, a green sprout starts popping through the ground. That seed has within it all the ingredients to become what it was meant to. When I plant a tomato seed, I truly expect it will be a tomato plant, and that in a few month's tomatoes will appear on the plant. It happens every time.

When you receive this free gift of salvation by faith, you repent because you know you have come short of God's glory. This seed of God begins to grow. It is no different than that tomato seed. When the seed of God impregnates you and me, we believe by faith that the Word says we are born again and have become a new creation. We have been forgiven of all our sins, our past, present and future sins.

Jesus died when He shed His blood; He did so for all of our sins. God has forgotten all our sin as it says in God's Word, *"You will cast all our sins into the depths of the sea"* (Micah 7:19). Also, Psalm 103:12 says, *"As far as the east is from the west, so far has He removed our transgressions from us."* Because of the power of the blood of Jesus to cleanse you and me, there has been placed upon us His robe of righteousness.

Unfortunately, many new spiritual babies don't pick up the Word and read it. You may go to a place of worship where God's people gather. The pastor or another mature leader will teach the Word and feed you but you will leave, and never pick up the Bible the rest of the week. If there is really no one in your life to disciple or mentor you, so you are able to grow up spiritually, you will basically starve for the rest of the week and wonder why nothing much is happening in your life. You are not watering your spirit with the Word of God. It's like a mother having a baby and putting it outside to fend for him or herself. The results will not be positive. The baby relies on the mother or someone to feed and nurture them, until they can manage to pick up the milk bottle themselves, or until the mother trains the baby to pick up a spoon to eat solid food.

3. WHAT IS WATER BAPTISM?

What does water baptism mean? The Greek word "baptizo" meant to dip, immerse, submerge. In secular Greek, it means to dip into a dye. It also means to draw water from a well with a pail, totally immersing the pail.

John the Baptist baptized people for the remission of their sins. But this was temporary until Jesus came. John declared that the kingdom of God at hand. Christian baptism is in the name of the Father, Son and

Holy Spirit. Christian baptism is to be permanent within the church. Christian baptism is into the death, burial, and resurrection of the Lord, and is an identification with Calvary's finished work. Baptism is not mere words or a formula into the name of the Lord Jesus Christ but rather it brings Christian believers to identify with Jesus Christ, as we also are buried with Him in baptism. Since I was buried in baptism, I no longer operate out of my old nature; it is gone, and I have come alive with a new nature through the resurrection of the Lord Jesus Christ. You and I now live and move and have our being in Jesus Christ.

ADDITIONAL READING: Matthew 3: 13–17; Mark 1:9 and Luke 3:7; Romans 6:4–11; Colossians 2:11–15.

In Acts 2:38, Peter told the Israelites to repent and be baptized in the name of Jesus Christ. Their response? "*Then those who gladly received his word were baptized; and that day about three thousand souls were added to them*" (Acts 2:41).

There are many other accounts of baptism in the book of Acts. See Acts 8:16 and Acts 10:44–48, Acts 19:4–5 for some examples.

To be baptized in water in the name of the Lord Jesus is significant in that when you were buried in the water, you actually were buried with Jesus Christ. Your identity is now in Jesus Christ. When you came out of the water, you arose in resurrection power with Christ. Your identity comes through baptism. Otherwise, how can you declare Galatians 2:20–21:

I have been crucified with Christ; it is no longer I who live, but Christ lives in me; and the life which I now live in the flesh I live by faith in the Son of God, who loved me and gave Himself for me. I do not set aside the grace of God; for if righteousness comes through the law, then Christ died in vain.

Taking these steps—repentance from dead works, faith in Jesus Christ, and then baptism in water in the name of the Lord Jesus—is a walk of obedience and identifying with Jesus Christ. Jesus walked in obedience to the Father's plan. I encourage you to trust God completely for this journey with Him. You will not be disappointed. Jesus died to redeem us.

4. WHAT DOES IT MEAN TO BE BAPTIZED IN THE HOLY SPIRIT?

True covenant relationship with Jesus Christ is expressed by the blood, water and the Spirit. The early church made it very clear that through repentance of sins, faith in Jesus Christ, baptism in water and the infilling of the Holy Spirit you identified with God and His plan and purpose for His people in the earth. These are just some of the doctrines of the Lord Jesus Christ as recorded in Hebrews 6:1–2.

Over time, we have developed many denominations that see baptism in different ways, following different traditions. But at the beginning, after the day of Pentecost, the apostles went out preaching and teaching the new covenant gospel according to what Jesus said and did while He was on earth. Jesus is, and shall always be, our true example in terms of new covenant relationship with Him. The gospel of Jesus Christ is free, but it will cost you and me by suffering for the truth of the gospel, which says you will have tribulation. Remember, we are in union with Jesus Christ. We have received and taken on His Nature, the old man is dead and the new creation is alive. Praise God!

As we delve into Holy Spirit baptism, note that Jesus told the disciples it was important for Him to go back to the Father, but not to be alarmed because He promised to send us the Comforter, the Holy Spirit. This is God expressing Himself in Spirit. God is Spirit; they that worship Him must worship in Spirit and in Truth. Jesus told the apostles to go up into the upper room and wait for the Holy Spirit, that they would know when He came for He would empower them with His Spirit. There was a mighty wind and tongues of fire over each one that gathered. The Spirit is often expressed through fire and wind in Scripture, and in this case both transpired. The Holy Spirit was released with the evidence of "speaking in other tongues." When you are born again, you are born of the Spirit. He is in you, but a releasing of the power for effective witness is through the evidence of you and me speaking in tongues. The Holy

Spirit will also help you live this life through Holy Spirit power and express your worship to the Lord.

Some of the greatest arguments and debates have arisen over this matter of the baptism of the Holy Spirit and speaking in tongues. Why do you suppose that is so? The key is the effectiveness of your witness with power. This message was spoken prophetically through Joel the prophet approximately 830 years prior to the birth of Jesus:

> *And it shall come to pass in the last days, says God, that I will pour out of My Spirit on all flesh; Your sons and your daughters shall prophesy, your young men shall see visions, your old men shall dream dreams. And on My menservants and on My maidservants I will pour out My Spirit in those days; and they shall prophesy. I will show wonders in heaven above and signs in the earth beneath: Blood and fire and vapor of smoke. The sun shall be turned into darkness, and the moon into blood, before the coming of the great and awesome day of the Lord. And it shall come to pass that whoever calls on the name of the Lord shall be saved.*
>
> —Acts 2:17–21

The last days began after Jesus went back to the Father. So here we are over two thousand years later, and the last days are much closer than when the church began.

We are living in exciting times, and these next few years are going to be the greatest times in history regarding millions coming in as the last–day harvest. We definitely need the power of the Holy Spirit released through a people who are open, and who will embrace all that God has given to us. Why would I shun this awesome gift of the baptism of the Holy Spirit? The Scripture says the traditions of man "*make the Word of God of no effect*" (Mark 7:13; see also 2 Peter 1:16-21). Let's not minimize this powerful gift of the Spirit. There comes a boldness, and an effective message to those who will hear. This has been God's plan long before and you and I were born. It was in the mind of God to make provision for us while we live this awesome life with Christ and are part of this great harvest.

The Holy Spirit is so much more than perhaps you and I have even considered, and He dwells in us as believers. The Names of the Holy Spirit reveal a balanced picture of His nature and ministry. Let's not underestimate His power.

Here are some examples to help you confirm in your spirit the value of the Holy Spirit:

- The Spirit – Genesis 1:2
- The Spirit of God – Matthew 3:16
- The Spirit of the Lord – 2 Corinthians 3:17
- The Spirit of the Father – Matthew 10:20
- The Spirit of Jesus Christ – Philippians 1:19
- The Spirit of Christ– Romans 8:9
- The Spirit of His Son – Galatians 4:6
- The Seven Spirits of God – Revelation 1:4; 4:5; 5:6
- The Spirit of Adoption – Romans 8:15
- The Spirit of Burning – Isaiah 4:4
- The Spirit of Faith – 2 Corinthians 4:13
- The Spirit of Glory – 1 Peter 4:14
- The Spirit of Grace – Zechariah 12:10; Hebrews 10:29
- The Spirit of Judgment – Isaiah 4:4; 28:6
- The Spirit of Life –Romans 8:2; Revelation 11:11
- The Spirit of Love – 2 Timothy 1:7
- The Spirit of Promise – Ephesians 1:13
- The Spirit of Prophecy – Revelation 19:10
- The Spirit of Revelation – Ephesians 1:17
- The Spirit of Truth – John 14:17; 15:26; 16:13; 1 John 5:6
- The Breath of the Almighty – Job 33:4
- The Comforter – John 14:16 and 26; 16:7
- The Power of the Highest – Luke 1:35
- An Unction from the Holy One –1 John 2:20

We cannot function without Him, for we are united with Christ and it is the Holy Spirit who teaches all things. He is equal with Father, and the Son, expressed through the Lord Jesus Christ.

It was predicted back in Isaiah 11:1–2 that the Messiah would be filled and anointed by the Holy Spirit:

There shall come forth a Rod from the stem of Jesse, and a Branch shall grow out of his roots. The Spirit of the Lord shall rest upon Him, the Spirit of wisdom and understanding, the Spirit of counsel and might, the Spirit of knowledge and of the fear of the Lord.

Isaiah 61:1–2 declares this about Jesus, the Messiah:

The Spirit of the Lord God is upon Me, because the Lord has anointed Me to preach good tidings to the poor; He has sent Me to heal the broken-hearted, to proclaim liberty to the captives, and the opening of the prison to those who are bound, to proclaim the acceptable year of the Lord....

This also was confirmed when Jesus picked up the scroll of Isaiah in the temple and began to confirm that it was He who was confirming the prophetic word spoken by Isaiah, something Peter later preached in Acts 10 (Luke 4:18–19; Acts 10:34–43).

Praise God! The mission of the Spirit could not begin until the earthly ministry of the Son had ended.

Reading John 14:15–21, we see Jesus say:

If you love Me, keep My commandments. And I will pray the Father, and He will give you another Helper, that He may abide with you for-ever—the Spirit of truth, whom the world cannot receive, because it neither sees Him nor knows Him; but you know Him, for He dwells with you and will be in you. I will not leave you orphans; I will come to you. A little while longer and the world will see Me no more, but you will see Me. Because I live, you will live also. At that day you will know that I am in My Father, and you in Me, and I in you. He who has My commandments and keeps them, it is he who loves Me. And he who loves Me will be loved by My Father, and I will love him and manifest Myself to him.

In the Old Testament, He dwells with you, and in the New Testament after Jesus' resurrection and ascension, He is in you. God's love for you and me is so outrageously awesome that He could not bear to let us fend for ourselves, but promised His Spirit would come into all who believe on Him. He also desires to release the Holy Spirit's power in and through you.

Baptism in water is a separate experience from Holy Spirit baptism. In fact, the day of Pentecost did not come until fifty days after Jesus ascended into heaven to the Father. Jesus knew how needful it would be for the disciples to have that power that He had. That power of God would impact lives as they preached the good news of the gospel of Jesus Christ, and His kingdom, the kingdom of God. God's power dwells in each one who opens up their heart and receives Him by faith.

I remember the day when I received the baptism of the Holy Spirit; it was like a dam broke inside me. The Word of God began to come alive; there was a clarity; the Word truly became alive to me and has done so ever since. If Jesus thought it necessary, how much more we too must embrace Holy Spirit.

Years after the day of Pentecost, Paul said this in 1 Corinthians 14:22, "*Therefore tongues are for a sign, not to those who believe but to unbelievers; but prophesying is not for unbelievers but for those who believe.*"

Jesus said:

> *And these signs will follow those who believe: in My name they will cast out demons; they will speak with new tongues; they will take up serpents; and if they drink anything deadly, it will by no means hurt them; they will lay hands on the sick, and they will recover.*
>
> —Mark 16:17–18

Don't seek the tongues, but seek the giver of the tongues. Worship Him and adore Him; tongues will follow. Paul in 1 Corinthians 14:18–19 gives wise counsel regarding tongues especially in a public place, "*I thank God I speak with tongues more than you all; yet in the church...*"

Keep in mind that Holy Spirit baptism is not an end; it is the gateway or beginning of a walk or a life in the Spirit. Another way of saying it is that the Holy Spirit baptism is a refreshing, as spoken in Isaiah 28:12. This Hebrew word means to rest, settle down, dwell, let fall, give comfort. Therefore, the Word reveals that we are to be a home, an abode, a mansion, or resting place for the Holy Spirit. The Holy Spirit comes upon the believer, and now He dwells within you as the temple.

As Jesus said, *"If anyone loves Me, he will keep My word; and My Father will love him, and We will come to him and make Our home with him"* (John 14:23). Let faith arise with the Word of God you have read, and surrender and receive this needful gift, a promise especially for you, so you can operate in the power of the Holy Spirit. It will change your life in a very special way.

Let's pray:

Jesus,
I thank you for your promise of sending the Holy Spirit. Your promise of power to be a witness is Your heart, Lord. I surrender and receive this gift now, and by faith I believe this gift is mine. Thank you. I worship You, I honour You, and glorify your Name. Amen.

ADDITIONAL READING: Acts 10:46; Acts 19:6; 1 Corinthians 12:10; Acts 1:8.

CHAPTER EIGHTEEN

The Feast of the Tabernacles

WE ARE IN A SEASON WHERE WE AWAIT JESUS' RETURN. IT IS THE TIME OF THE end–time harvest. As we await his return, we are to repent and believe and prepare the Bride of Christ. This season is characterized by seven different things:

I. UNITY

In John 17:11, there is a cry from Jesus to the Father, "*...that they may be one, as We are.*" David the Psalmist sang this song in Psalm 133:1–3:

> *Behold, how good and how pleasant it is for brethren to dwell together in unity! It is like the precious oil upon the head, running down on the beard, the beard of Aaron, running down on the edge of his garments. It is like the dew of Hermon, descending upon the mountains of Zion; for there the Lord commanded the blessing—Life forevermore.*

As we consider what this concept of unity is all about, our focus should be always toward Jesus Christ. If we try to make unity happen from a place of the flesh, greater division will ensue. The cry of Jesus' heart for oneness with Him and the Father is His hope for all who walk in unity by faith. God's heart is to bring blessing. Let's choose to operate out of God's heart.

Being around the church community for most of my life, I am very well aware of prejudice that has lurked around. Prejudice is anything that separates us from God and each other. Prejudice is also a learned behaviour. Prejudice comes from and is based upon the spirit of fear, underlined by insecurity and fear of rejection. It comes from a heart of pride and arrogance. It has built many walls in the body of Christ and should not be there since we are representatives of the kingdom of God. When prejudice prevails, God's love is not in action through us.

Prejudice is a pre–judgment call on a situation before the facts are known. It is bigotry, discrimination, intolerance, narrow–mindedness, partiality. Prejudice is poison. Those words are from the fleshly realm. I believe it is why the church has issues that are not manifesting the heart of Jesus Christ. We must recognize that the enemy has pulled a major attack against the Church, but as the Church begins to recognize this, the spirit of repentance will bring about a change of mind toward a spirit of unity in Christ.

The greatest prejudice I encountered was denominational prejudice. I grew up in this kind of environment. There always seemed to be the great divide. Why would anyone even want to believe Jesus is the answer when all the world can see is a skewed view of who Jesus is? God is love, and He commands us to love one another. Sometimes we say, I love you only if you come over to my denomination. We may have been well intentioned, but this is totally contrary to God's heart. I found myself repenting and asking Him to change my heart and mind. That has been one of the major changes I have seen in my life regarding church community. I am now able to see my brother and sister in Christ with the heart and love of God, with His help and grace. If we want to really find the answers, we will find God's heart in the Word of God, the Bible.

The only remedy for this universal human need is the personal and collective experience of the love of God—being forgiven, accepted in the Beloved, safe and secure in Christ. As Galatians 3:28 teaches, "*There is neither Jew nor Greek, there is neither slave nor free, there is neither male nor female; for you are all one in Christ Jesus.*"

That is why there is no need to demonstrate prejudice, for we are all one in Christ Jesus. My prayer for you, the reader, is that you will allow the Spirit of God in you to do that good work, until Christ is fully formed in you (Galatians 4:19).

I challenge you to consider listening to God's heart, surrender to Him any prejudices in the areas of gender, race, denomination, wealth, politics, etc. Open your heart to be delivered from prejudice this day forward, and desire the unity of the spirit.

ADDITIONAL READING: Leviticus 23:33–43; 1 Corinthians 1:10; 2 Corinthians 2:13–16; 1Corinthians 12:13–14; Ephesians 4.

2. JOY FOR THE HARVEST

As the Holy Spirit is working in all of us, the greatest joy should be to see the harvest of souls coming in. That has always been God's heart, and particularly now in this season as the Day of the Lord draws near. Unfortunately, I have seen, in the past twenty years especially, a non–caring attitude toward the unsaved. The church in general has become lethargic to the point of prejudice. But something is stirring in the spirit realm where attitudes are changing, mindsets are opening up once again for the heart of the Father. Great joy is becoming explosive in people's lives as they awaken to see the need of the harvest to come in. He is calling the young and the older generations.

We can share in the joy of the angels: "*Likewise, I say to you, there is joy in the presence of the angels of God over one sinner who repents*" (Luke 15:10).

Sometimes joy is hard. In the psalms that are the songs of ascents, the people of Israel were in captivity, captive to a sense of hopelessness, bitterness, anger, and lost dreams; then God appeared to His people, and a heart of laughter, and singing, and joy returned. They declared "*The Lord has done great things for us and we are glad*" (Psalm 126:3). Hope was arising once again, faith to their God, the God of Israel. Then in verse five and six, this came statement: "*Those who sow in tears shall reap in joy. He who continually goes forth weeping, bearing seed for sowing, shall doubtless come again with rejoicing, bringing his sheaves with him.*"

I am sure many of us have gone through the deep dark places of the soul where all you feel is hopelessness. Nothing seems to be happening. The desire to love one another, and compassion for lost souls, begins to wane. Discouragement may come, but God's Word will never fail, because

His Word is eternal. There is a season in our lives for God to test our hearts, and when He keeps telling you He loves you, and nothing changes, regardless, we still hold to His Word, for He promises us He will never leave us or forsake us. Just remember our priority is Jesus and His plan for mankind. He loves His creation, and is not willing that any should perish, but that all should come to repentance and faith toward God. Our heart becomes God's heart of compassion for those who still need to come into the kingdom of God for such a time as this. *"No one can come to Me unless the Father who sent Me draws him; and I will raise him up at the last day"* (John 6:44).

ADDITIONAL READING: Isaiah 65:17–25

3. INGATHERING OF THE FINAL HARVEST

As I write this section, I feel an excitement in the spirit to once again hope and confidently trust God that the harvest is upon us. In some parts of the earth, there are thousands upon thousands coming to Christ. Spiritual eyes are being opened. I rejoice with them. As we embrace the harvest, there is a people in the earth whom Holy Spirit has been working on to have the passion of the Father to see the great ingathering like never seen before.

In Exodus 23:16, the Feast of Harvest and the Feast of Ingathering was a most wonderful time, when the work of their labours meant gathering the fruit and produce in.

In John 15:1–2, Jesus speaks of the true vine and the Father is the vinedresser. *"Every branch in Me that does not bear fruit He takes away; and every branch that bears fruit He prunes, that it may bear more fruit"* (John 15:2).

Now you can see the heart of the Father and the Son. Pruning is and has been necessary so that nothing can come in the way of the harvest. If you feel like your wings have been clipped for a season, they were being clipped for a reason. God's love is beyond measure. Don't fight it, but embrace the discipline of the Lord so that more fruit will come forth. This fruit is Christ in you, the hope of glory. The glory of God was so strong and bright on Peter that when he walked by the people his shadow actually healed them.

4. REST

You and I have to stop striving from the attitude that says, "I have to do this or do that, otherwise God will not be pleased. After all, I want the 'crown' at the end." It is not about "I." it is about Christ in you, and Him coming forward for the world to see. It is about just being who God planned for you to be. Allow His character, His heart, His love, His grace, His mercy to be expressed in you, and see how restful that experience is. He is our rest, and peace and joy. You have no need to be going after "the works" stuff. The old nature is dead, and you are alive with His resurrection power dwelling in you.

Hear what God says about this: "*There remains therefore a rest for the people of God. For he who has entered His rest has himself also ceased from his works as God did from His*" (Hebrews 4:9). We now just rest in Him, our Lord. This is what Jesus paid for—that rest—to redeem us. There is no reason to panic and live with anxiety. It is a matter of trusting God through this process of true rest, via His Word and wisdom.

Paul writes:

For this reason I bow my knees to the Father of our Lord Jesus Christ, from whom the whole family in heaven and earth is named, that He would grant you, according to the riches of His glory, to be strengthened with might through His Spirit in the inner man, that Christ may dwell in your hearts through faith; that you, being rooted and grounded in love, may be able to comprehend with all the saints what is the width and length and depth and height—to know the love of Christ which passes knowledge; that you may be filled with all the fullness of God. Now to Him who is able to do exceedingly abundantly above all that we ask or think, according to the power that works in us, to Him be glory in the church by Christ Jesus to all generations, forever and ever. Amen.
—Ephesians 3:14–21

This is why you and I can rest in these days. It's not about the laws we have to keep, for this mystery proclaims Christ in you with His strength and His power, until we are filled with all the fullness of God. When we pray for Holy Spirit to do that good work of His grace in us, remember verse twenty. He is able to do exceedingly abundantly above all that we ask or think. He will never give up on you, God's love is eternal, His love will never stop. So rest!

When the world out there sees this rest in your life, the world will see God's glory, His grace, His love. For you and I know how much unrest is swirling about us. There is this Scripture I want us to be reminded of again:

> *Little children, let no one deceive you. He who practices righteousness is righteous, just as He is righteous. He who sins is of the devil, for the devil has sinned from the beginning. For this purpose the Son of God was manifested, that He might destroy the works of the devil. Whoever has been born of God does not sin, for His seed remains in him; and he cannot sin, because he has been born of God.*
>
> —1 John 3:7–9

In this Scripture above, you can rest. Jesus has destroyed the works of the devil; we just have to believe it, and our responses in this life come out of His rest. His finished work is final and secure.

ADDITIONAL READING: Leviticus 23:39; 2 Chronicles 6:12–42.

5. GLORY

In the month of March 2016, I had a vision while in prayer. In the vision, I saw a person who was very tall. This form was shimmering against the darkened backdrop of the evening. As this person kept walking closer toward me, the brightness increased. The shimmering told me that person was very much alive, and expressed great strength and power and overwhelming brightness. As the person drew nearer, I had this sense of the fear and awe of God. I desired to bow in honour of Him.

As I asked the Lord what this meant, I heard Holy Spirit say, "This is the remnant with Jesus the head. This is the remnant who has been willing to follow my discipline, and who walk in obedience. They know my love, and they have united with Me as one. They are the united remnant who shine forth my glory. They are the ones who will gather in my harvest field."

It made me think of the book of Daniel where Daniel writes, "*Those who are wise shall shine like the brightness of the firmament, and those who turn many to righteousness like the stars forever and ever*" (Daniel 12:3) and "*Many shall be purified, made white, and refined; but the wicked shall do wickedly; and none of the wicked shall understand, but the wise shall understand*" (Daniel 12:10).

The glory is who God is. His glory is expressed in power, brightness, character; folks, it's not about us, it's truly all about Him. God clothed Himself in flesh when He was born of the Virgin Mary. He went back to the Father and has clothed Himself now in flesh through His Body, the Church. We are the honoured vehicle in which Christ shines forth. You and I will discover as we bring in the harvest field, families, and even cities will be saved. We have entered into the moment for the harvest to be gathered.

When I grew up on the farm, harvest was an exciting time. There were a few weeks to gather in the fields of wheat, barley, rye, oats, or whatever Dad and my brothers had sowed into the ground in the spring. The storehouses were prepared, and when it was time to gather, the whole family was involved. I remember when I was about ten years old, I would shovel the wheat into the corners of the five–tonne truck. We worked from morning till seven or eight in the evening sometimes. Mom seemed to be cooking continuously to feed the hungry mouths. We were one busy family when it was harvest. I remember Dad checking the heads of grain every day to see if it was too damp or just the right dryness. Timing was everything in harvesting the grain.

Even as you read this today, I pray a stirring and compassion will come in your spirit like never before, to see this end-time harvest brought in. Pray the Lord of the harvest to send out labourers into His harvest. Will you be a willing labourer?

ADDITIONAL READING: Matthew 9:37–38, Luke 10, 1 Samuel 4:21–22; Hebrews 7; 1 Peter 2:9; Zechariah 6:13; Joel 2:1–2; 1 Kings 8:1–11; Isaiah 40:1–5; John 17.

6. RESTORATION

God is in the business of restoration. It is a theme in the book of Ezra during the reign of Cyrus, King of Persia. So that Jeremiah's prophesy might be fulfilled, King Cyrus decreed that the Lord God of heaven has given to me to *"build Him a house at Jerusalem, which is in Judah"* (2 Chronicles 36:23).

The heads of the fathers of Judah and Benjamin and the priests and the Levites, with all whose spirits God had moved, arose to go up and build the house of the Lord which was in Jerusalem. Included in the whole assembly of 42,360, besides their male and female servants, and with the priests and Levites, were singers (200 male and female singers), gatekeepers, and the Nethinim (temple servants), and many animals. When the foundation was being built, the priests began to play the trumpets and cymbals to praise God. *"For He is good, for His mercy endures forever toward Israel"* (Ezra 3:11).

Praise and worship was deemed of utmost importance as part of the building of the temple, and according to the ordinance of David King of Israel. They also kept the Feast of Tabernacles and daily burnt offerings as required.

As God is building Himself in us, worship takes priority. We express our heart of gratitude, love and adoration to the God who has delivered us from captivity and bondage from sin.

The adversary, Satan, hates our worship to God who is our deliverer. But we can stand firm, just as in Ezra, when adversaries were resisting the building of the temple, and Zerubbabel and the rest of the leaders said, *"You may do nothing with us to build a house for our God; but we alone will build to the Lord God of Israel, as King Cyrus has commanded us"* (Ezra 4:3). The adversaries tried to discourage the people of Judah, by frustrating their purpose.

Here is a warning, that we do not fall into the enemy's trap: align yourself with God's vision rather than with people who will try to have other alternatives and motives. And know that even though so much discouragement came, and the work was halted for a season, when King Darius took over, the Israelites resumed the building of the temple (Nehemiah 1–13). God is always faithful. As you read Isaiah 42 and the book of Zechariah, you see the heart of God, who longs to see His people restored.

7. APPEARING OF THE LORD IN THE CHURCH AND THEN IN THE AIR

When I was a very young girl, I was trained by my parents and church that Jesus could come at any minute. We were told to keep ourselves from the world, have nothing to do with it, and hang out only with believers in Jesus. This was drilled into my head fifty–plus years ago. Over the years I realized Jesus is going to appear, but first in His church, and then in the air.

There is a key chapter in John 7. It was during the beginning of the Feast of Tabernacles. Jesus told his brothers to go to the feast in Judea for His time was not yet fully come. Jesus stayed back in Galilee. Why? The Jews hated Him and had it in their hearts to kill Jesus for He had been preaching things contrary to the Jewish belief system in terms of the law. In verse five, it says, *"for even His brothers did not believe in Him."* Sometime later, Jesus arrived in Judea quietly and secretively. Jesus heard some good, and some very contrary comments about Himself. They claimed Jesus was deceiving people. Later Jesus went to the temple and began to teach there. The Jews marveled at Him for He knew much doctrine, but had never studied. Then Jesus declared the following:

> *My doctrine is not Mine, but His who sent Me. If anyone wills to do His will, he shall know concerning the doctrine, whether it is from God or whether I speak on My own authority. He who speaks from himself seeks his own glory; but He who seeks the glory of the One who sent Him is true, and no unrighteousness is in Him. Did not Moses give you the law, yet none of you keeps the law? Why do you seek to kill Me?*
> —John 7:17–19

Much talk went about, and questioned this episode. Finally He said to them:

> *I shall be with you a little while longer, and then I go to Him who sent Me. You will seek Me and not find Me, and where I am you cannot come.*
>
> —John 7:33–34

The Jews were in a quandary and questioned the statement. Finally, Jesus made this powerful statement regarding the promise of the Holy Spirit: "*If anyone thirsts, let him come to Me and drink. He who believes in Me as the Scripture has said, out of his heart will flow rivers of living water*" (John 7:37).

The Spirit of God would come after Jesus went away back to the Father. As you can very well see, even as Jesus was sent by the Father, we too are sent, via the Holy Spirit with Jesus our Head and we as His Body. We represent the Lord Jesus as ambassadors to witness to the world, who still need to hear the good news of the gospel; we truly are honoured and privileged. Jesus promised He would not leave us comfortless but that His spirit would be in us, He operates in and through us as the vessel, expressing this wonderful message of hope:

> *Behold what manner of love the Father has bestowed on us, that we should be called children of God! Therefore, the world does not know us, because it did not know Him. Beloved, now we are children of God; and it has not yet been revealed what we shall be, but we know that when He is revealed, we shall be like Him, for we shall see Him as He is. And everyone who has this hope in Him purifies himself, just as He is pure.*
>
> —1 John 3:1–3

As you can see in the above verses, as we have this hope in Him we purify ourselves, just as He is pure. It is necessary in God's awesome plan to demonstrate Himself through a people who are willing to surrender all to the Lordship of Jesus. For Paul declared in Galatians 4:19, "*...I labor in birth again until Christ is formed in you.*" As you allow faith and hope to work in you, Christ will continuously come forth more and more until the world will see the glory of Jesus. As I said earlier in the book regarding the divine nature of God in us and through us, this is that witness. Jesus is growing and growing in us, and this is the appearing of the Lord "in us."

ADDITIONAL READING: 2 Peter 1:16–21; Colossians 3:1–4; Romans 12:1–2; 2 Corinthians 3:15–18; Revelation 11 and 12.

It is so important not to diminish the appearing of the Lord in the air. There is something so important to keep in mind regarding the Lord's desires, for He said He is coming for a church without spot or wrinkle. The Christ being formed in all believers is very significant, preparing us before He returns in the air. There is something about the whole earth being filled with His glory as the waters cover the sea. His glory is coming out of a people who are willing to let the Holy Spirit do that work in our soul realm, until Christ is formed in all of us who believe. Our spirit is saved, our soul is being saved and our body shall be saved, transformed from corruptible to an incorruptible body.

When I was very young and up to my late twenties, I was under the impression Jesus was coming through the Rapture at any minute. I could not figure out how He said He was coming for a church without spot or wrinkle if He could be coming at any moment. I lived in fear for many of my former years even though I was a believer. I remember a man stood up in a church I was attending back in the 1980s and he said Jesus was coming by the end of the year and strongly warned us. Then I realized that Satan was using that tactic to put fear in people. This man lived another twenty–five years and Jesus did not come in the air to take us out of here.

Is He coming? Yes of course. Why? The Word of God tells us.

As you listen to the news, the *"wars and rumours of wars"* spoken of in Matthew 24 seem to be becoming more and more real. The disciples asked Jesus one day while they sat on the Mount of Olives, what would be the sign of His coming, and of the end of the age? Jesus' first response was quite clear, *"Take heed that no one deceives you. For many will come in My name, saying 'I am the Christ'"* (Matthew 24:4–5). He then added more details about His coming:

- You will hear of wars and rumours of wars. Do not be troubled. For this must happen, but the end is not yet.
- Nation will rise against nation, kingdom against kingdom.
- There will be famines, pestilences, and earthquakes in various places. But this is the beginning of sorrows.
- You will be delivered up to tribulation and kill you, and you will be hated of all nations for My name's sake.
- Many will be offended, betray one another.
- Many false prophets will rise up and deceive many.
- Because of lawlessness, the love of many will grow cold.
- He who endures to the end shall be saved.
- This gospel of the kingdom will be preached in all the world as a witness to all the nations, and then the end will come.

You can read the rest of Matthew 24, noting especially verses thirty-four and thirty-five where Jesus says:

Assuredly, I say to you, this generation will by no means pass away till all these things take place. Heaven and earth will pass away, but My words will by no means pass away.

In 1 Thessalonians 2:19–20, Paul is describing to the church how he so wanted to come, but Satan hindered him:

For what is our hope, or joy, or crown of rejoicing? Is it not even you in the presence of our Lord Jesus Christ at his coming? For you are our glory and joy.

By this time Jesus had gone back to the Father when He ascended not long before the day of Pentecost. Paul now reminding that Jesus was coming back in the future. Paul continues to say a prayer for the Church in 1 Thessalonians 3:11–13:

Now may our God and Father Himself, and our Lord Jesus Christ, direct our way to you. And may the Lord make you increase and bound in love to one another and to all, just as we do to you, so that He may establish your hearts blameless in holiness before our God and Father at the coming of our Lord Jesus Christ with all His saints.

1 Thessalonians 4:13–18 describes the end-times:

But I do not want you to be ignorant, brethren, concerning those who have fallen asleep, lest you sorrow as others who have no hope. For if we believe that Jesus died and rose again, even so God will bring with Him those who sleep in Jesus. For this we say to you by the word of the Lord, that we who are alive and remain until the coming of the Lord will by no means precede those who are asleep. For the Lord Himself will descend from heaven with a shout, with the voice of an archangel, and with the trumpet of God. And the dead in Christ will rise first. Then we who are alive and remain shall be caught up together with them in the clouds to meet the Lord in the air. And thus we shall always be with the Lord. Therefore, comfort one another with these words.

The Bible talks about the spirit of antichrist that is still prevailing in the world (1 John 2:18–19). I am not here to put fear in you, but to make you aware that this is happening and will happen, to remind you not to lose heart, troubled or shaken in mind. Remember the Holy Anointed One lives and dwells within you. Jesus promised His peace to us. Do not embrace fear, but have faith in the Son of God, who is Jesus who has redeemed you. You are His.

We are living in a time where patience and perseverance is required as you embrace Jesus Christ and refuse to be moved by anything that may come your way:

Who shall separate us from the love of Christ? Shall tribulation, or distress, or persecution, or famine, or nakedness, or peril, or sword? As it is written: "For Your sake we are killed all day long; we are accounted as sheep for the slaughter."

—Romans 8:35–36

James teaches us to be prepared:

Therefore be patient, brethren, until the coming of the Lord. See how the farmer waits for the precious fruit of the earth, waiting patiently for it until it receives the early and latter rain. You also be patient. Establish your hearts, for the coming of the Lord is at hand.

—James 5:7–8

The key during these times of difficulty is to abide in Him. As John writes:

And now, little children, abide in Him, that when He appears, we may have confidence and not be ashamed before Him at His coming. If you know that He is righteous, you know that everyone who practices righteousness is born of Him.

—1 John 2:28–29

One final verse, 1 John 3:1–3:

Behold what manner of love the Father has bestowed on us, that we should be called children of God! Therefore, the world does not know us, because it did not know Him. Beloved, now we are children of God; and it has not yet been revealed what we shall be, but we know that when He is revealed, we shall be like Him, for we shall see Him as He is. And everyone who has this hope in Him purifies himself, just as He is pure.

I really want to encourage to take hope in our God. He said it: it is done. Let your faith embrace this season, being fully confident that what He says, He will fulfill.

We are living in the most tremendous times where we will see the former and latter reign come together to bring in this end–time harvest of souls. We are truly in a blessed season of time. Except the Lord build this house, they labour in vain who build.

Therefore, go and make disciples!

CHAPTER NINETEEN

Prayer is the Key

I SEE THE LORD JESUS BENDING HIS EAR TO OUR HEART AS WE CRY OUT FOR mercy and grace and forgiveness:

> Revival should be the cry of our hearts, but even more, I pray for a "habitation" for You, Lord, in our hearts, both personally and corporately. For You are building a permanent dwelling place where You shine forth like a city set on a hill. Where Your glory shines so brightly that the whole earth is filled with Your glory, Your glory in us.
>
> Lord Jesus, come and dwell in us, your people, where every room of this building cannot contain it all but must be poured out on the streets of our cities, towns and villages. For, Lord, You say in Your Word that those whom the Lord loves, He disciplines. We embrace Your discipline today: burn all the dross out of my life until You are fully and completely formed in me. Your character and lifestyle, your words, your heart pours out in intercession for a people who still must come into the kingdom of God for such a time as this. Shine, Jesus, shine, brighter and brighter each day that I live on this earth. Shine so bright that the world will declare and say "Who is that Jesus that dwells in you?" We will declare God's greatness and power, His holiness and majesty.
>
> Lord, shake us until we can say and mean it, "I have been crucified with Christ; it is no longer I who live, but Christ

lives in me; and the life which I now live in the flesh I live by faith of the Son of God, who loved me and gave Himself for me."(Galatians 2:20)

Lord, let us love like You love. Let us give like You give. Let us extend grace like You extend grace. Let us extend mercy like You extend mercy. Rip out every bit of prejudice that is in me. None of me but all of You, Lord.

I see a Body running the race where every part is needed. A Body that can't help itself in spreading Your love, Lord. You are the head, Lord, and I acknowledge your headship over Your people. We are bringing heaven down to earth through the manifestation of the sons of God. Enlarge and increase Yourself in us until, Jesus, you manifest Yourself through a fully surrendered Body.

Lord hear our prayer, our cry. Be exalted in the earth and let the whole earth hear Your thunderous voice, Your gentle heart, Your abundance of peace and joy. Holy, Holy is the Lord! Amen.

In keeping with this theme of prayer, I am reminded of the fact that when you or I love someone, we want to hang around with them as much as possible. Jesus is attached to us, His Body. He longs for a people to spend time with Him continuously. Everywhere you go, whether at work or shopping or play, He loves communing with us. I encourage you to spend time with Him 24–7. When you plan a trip, go to the Lord for His wisdom. When changing jobs, take the concern to Him. Pray for your children and your grandchildren. Pray and talk to the Lord regarding your business. Pray together with family. Pray together in groups. Put Jesus in the forefront of your daily life so you will learn to listen to His voice, and so that when He speaks, you will immediately recognize His voice.

Even after years and years of not hearing or seeing some of your family, you still will recognize their voices. Recently, I made contact with a cousin of mine whom I hadn't heard from since we were sixteen. Fifty–plus years later when I spoke with her on the phone I still recognized her voice. I still remember my sister's voice as we talked at least once or twice a week for years and years. She passed away six months ago. There is a fine–tuning that happens when you spend time with Jesus. There is that certain sound of voice that won't let you forget His voice. The more time we spend waiting on the Lord, through meditation, prayer and the reading and studying of the Word of God, the more clearly we will hear His voice. For me, His voice oozes with love, for God is love. The more time I spend with Him, the more I long to hear His voice, and the clearer His voice becomes to me.

Recently I was asked to go pray with a sister in the Lord for a cousin who was dying in the hospital. When we arrived, the room was filled with relatives. At one point I was asked if I would pray for this man. His eyes were closed, and by the sound of his breathing I sensed he might not be with us for long. I did not have a clue how I should pray for him. I heard in my spirit that I should ask for Jesus to reveal Himself in a dream or vision so this man, if he had never accepted Christ, would do it before he left this earth. I had such peace when I was finished that I knew the Lord heard my prayer and He was going to minister to this man in a very real way. One thing I remember specifically was the clarity of the Lord's voice when He gave me instructions. God is good, and I am expecting to see that man one day, in the heavenly realm. In part of this Scripture it says, *"For to be absent from this body and to be present with the Lord"* (2 Corinthians 5:1–8).

When Nehemiah found out about the Jews who had survived captivity, whose wall had broken down and who were in much distress. Nehemiah said, *"I sat down and wept and mourned for many days; I was fasting and praying before the God of heaven"* (Nehemiah 1:4). Nehemiah was overcome with compassion for those Jews. He responded with weeping, fasting and prayer. Do you and I do likewise when we see a need?

As we consider the call to reach out to those who still need to hear the gospel, are our hearts desperate enough to see help and compassion come from God to them? Oh Lord, forgive their sins and heal them, O God! Do we cry out for their salvation and deliverance?

In Isaiah 56, the prophet cries out to the Lord regarding the Gentiles and says in verse 7–8:

Even them I will bring to My holy mountain, and make them joyful in my house of prayer. Their burnt offerings and their sacrifices will be accepted on My altar; for my house shall be called a house of prayer for all nations. The Lord God, who gathers the outcasts of Israel, says, Yet I will gather to him others besides those who are gathered to him.

If it was good enough for Isaiah, we should make prayer a priority before anything else we do.

In all the gospels, we see that prayer was a highly important part of Jesus' life He spent much time alone, praying to the Father.

ADDITIONAL READING: 1 Thessalonians 5:17; 2 Timothy 1:3; Romans 1:9, James 5:16.

Finally, there is a Scripture in 2 Chronicles that I have heard for as long as I can remember. It is a call to repentance, for our land. The Lord desires salvation to come to all who will be willing to hear the word of the Lord.

If My people who are called by My name will humble themselves, and pray and seek My face, and turn from their wicked ways, then I will hear from heaven, and will forgive their sin and heal their land.
—2 Chronicles 7:14

I pray our hearts will remain tender, and that we will believe the Word of God and His promises to us, and believe what God says He would do. His promise is sure.

In closing, if we expect to see the end–time harvest come in, repentance and prayer and seeking the Lord with all your heart will be the keys to unlocking this season and experiencing the manifestation of souls coming into the kingdom of God for such a time as this. This is God's plan and purpose and vision. Let's embrace Him, for Jesus is not willing that any should perish, but that all should come to repentance, and then to experience the intimacy of relationship with an eternal God who loves us with an everlasting love. So be it!

Testimony

I was raised in a Christian home in the province of Saskatchewan. By the time I reached the age of five, the Holy Spirit spoke to me about receiving Jesus Christ as my personal Saviour. The catalyst was my sister and two brothers coming home one day from Vacation Bible School saying they had all accepted Jesus Christ into their hearts. I began to cry and said to my mother, "Mom, I want Jesus in my heart too." So, my mother led me to Jesus.

At the age of twelve I was water–baptized and filled with the Holy Spirit that same summer.

When I graduated from high school, I went to Saskatoon to work. I also met my future husband and was married in 1966. We had three children together and I now have nine grandchildren.

Prayer and study of the Word have always been a big part of my life, and I have grown in the Lord.

Although friends and family have said for a few years now that I should be retired, I find that my writing, discipling believers, and being in involved in a number of work-related projects open doors in different arenas providing a mission field of sharing the good news of the gospel. Have you heard the statement, "Bloom where you are planted?" That is what I'm trying to do.

I am believing the light of God's glory continues to shine brighter and brighter in my life no matter where I go each day. That is my prayer for you.

—Olivia McClure